Almost Home

Almost Home

a memoir

Hilary Harper

Tree Garden Press

Published by Tree Garden Press
Copyright © 2017 Hilary Harper
All rights reserved.

ISBN-13: 9780998626208
ISBN-10: 0998626201
Library of Congress Control Number: 2017905177
Hilary Harper, Huntington Woods, MI

Quotation from When We Were Orphans by Kazuo Ishiguro, published by
Faber & Faber, 2000, copyright Kazuo Ishiguro, reproduced by permission of
the author c/o Rogers, Coleridge & White Ltd., 20 Powis Mews, London W11
IJN

*For anyone, and everyone, who has ever longed to know
who they are*

When I imagine the night my mother and her sister died, I see them speeding down a California highway in a car with the radio on. The accident happened in 1955, so I see them in one of those big rounded sedans of the time, a car without seatbelts. I imagine them laughing, the car windows open to the warm night air, and I imagine they'd all been drinking, including the sailor behind the wheel. Though I could be wrong about that. I must have been asleep in my crib when the car and a truck collided at 12:45 a.m. A seven-month-old "illegitimate" infant, I was taken in by a childless couple who let me believe they were my parents.

Part One

CHAPTER 1

Something Significant

I run to the car where my mom is waiting at the end of every school day. Lugging my big leather book bag, I open the passenger door and slide in next to her on the wide front seat. After an eight-hour shift of soldering radiator parts she is weary, but glad to see me, her only child. The scent of hot metal lingers on her clothes, and she might have a candy bar for me in her pocket, a Butterfinger or a Baby Ruth.

The ride to our house takes only a few minutes if we don't have to wait for a train or stop at the store, and when we get there I plop down in front of the TV while my mom goes into the kitchen to make dinner. While waiting for something to simmer or bake, she sits at our chrome-legged table reading the paper, doing the crossword, and chain-smoking menthol Kools.

I grew up in Wyandotte, a blue-collar suburb southwest of Detroit. And when I recall an ordinary day in my childhood, I recall the comfort of being at home in the late afternoon. Our house, a Craftsman bungalow, had oak woodwork, hardwood floors, an art deco chandelier in the dining room, and a two-car garage. My parents purchased the house in 1957 with cash, ten thousand dollars they saved up—an example of what the labor unions made possible. A working man or woman in Detroit could enjoy a middle-class lifestyle and look forward to a middle-class retirement, even if they were unskilled and hadn't graduated from high school.

We lived on the corner of Third and Cedar, and next door to us lived the Affholters, a family with five boys. I was the same age as the middle Affholter boy, Jerry, and we were always running around together. We raced bicycles, built snow forts, played hide-and-seek, tag, and war. Our block was our world, and it seemed a vast territory.

I remember my life in the early 1960s as carefree and idyllic despite the ordeal of parochial school. I was a Polish Catholic girl whose parents worked in factories—my dad at a steel mill and my mom at a place that made tractor and truck parts. And I accepted this as naturally as anyone accepts the circumstances into which they are born.

My earliest memory is of my teenage cousin, Andy Kwiatkowski, hoisting me up onto his shoulders so I could touch the ceilings in all the rooms of our house on Cedar Street. I remember the pure delight of this. As the youngest of my cousins, I got a lot of attention at family gatherings, many of which were held at our house.

My mom put the leaf in the dining room table for parties and holidays, and this would be where everyone gathered to eat, gossip, laugh, and play cards. "High-low," one of my uncles might say as he shuffled and dealt amid cigar smoke and the clink of coins being thrown in the poker pot. "Jacks or better," another might announce. It fascinated me when players threw their cards down in disgust or raked in a big pile of money with glee. I would worm my way onto someone's lap to watch, my lips stained red from drinking cherry-flavored pop.

Adored and indulged by my family as a young child, I had a hard time adjusting to the discipline of school. Reading came easily to me, but I had no interest in memorizing facts or doing my homework—a fault that exasperated the nuns. Felician sisters in full black habits with starched white wimples, the nuns at Our Lady of Mt. Carmel were as stern as their stereotype.

By second grade my high self-esteem had plummeted. Frequently scolded in class, I also had the strangest name. The only other Hilary most people had ever heard of then was Sir Edmund Hillary, the explorer, but he was a man and that was his *last* name.

My mom had nicknamed me Lori—a nice, ordinary 1960s girl's name. Everyone I knew called me Lori, and I expected to be called Lori at school. But the nuns insisted I go by my baptismal name: Hilary Bocianowski. A horrible, alien name. Lori was *me,* an essential part of my identity. Hilary became my miserable alter-ego. The miserable me at school.

One night, while my mom stood at the stove, busy with something sizzling in a cast iron skillet—pork chops maybe, or pierogies with onions—I asked why she named me Hilary.

"I don't know," she said in an offhand way. "I guess I just thought it was a good name."

"So, why do you call me Lori?"

She moved the food around in the pan and began to sing.

"Lori, Lori, bo-bori, banana fanna fo fori…"

"Mom!" I protested.

"Fee-fi mo mori..."

My mom, Marie, often sang in the kitchen. Mostly songs from the 1940s, like "Chattanooga Choo Choo," "Sentimental Journey," and "Mairzy Doats" (my favorite). She also whistled while she cooked or washed the dishes, a skill I admired since I couldn't whistle at all, no matter how hard I tried.

Like most kids, I asked my mom a lot of questions. And when she was too distracted or too tired to answer, she would shoo me away. "Get outta my hair now," she'd say in a gentle way.

The Affholter family moved in 1964, a traumatic event for me. Those boys were as close as I came to having siblings. They had been a part of my life for as long as I could remember. But they ran out of space in their house soon after Mrs. Affholter had her seventh son. They moved four blocks away, which might as well have been the moon. The Affholters were *gone*, and a part of me went with them. I rode my bike that summer without enthusiasm and played hopscotch all by myself.

Then one day I met a girl named Cathy at Jaycee Park, our neighborhood playground.

She was pushing an old blue baby carriage, with an actual baby inside it. She rolled the carriage up to the swings and removed her youngest sibling, Jack, a one-year-old wearing only a diaper and shoes. An outgoing girl with her blonde hair in braids, Cathy sat next to me on the swings and said, "Hi."

"Hi," I said.

She was exactly one month older than me, went to public school, lived two blocks away, and had six younger siblings. *Another big family!* We soon became best friends and developed the kind of devoted relationship young girls often form. We began spending as much time together as possible, except for going to different schools, which was fine with me since it kept Cathy from knowing my Hilary persona.

In the spring of 1967, Cathy and I were twelve years old. We were out of school for the week of Easter, and since both of my parents were at work, we had my house to ourselves. I tuned the radio to our favorite hit station and we practiced dancing in front of my mom's bedroom mirror. We might have been listening to "I'm a Believer" by the Monkees or "Somebody to Love" by Jefferson Airplane when we began opening my mom's dresser drawers. I liked to snoop, but felt ashamed of myself because of it. It seemed less wrong when there were two of us doing it. We both liked pretending we were looking for clues, like Nancy Drew.

After examining the dresser and not finding anything of interest except some old garter belts, I crossed the room and opened the cedar-lined window seat—a built-in compartment below the bedroom windows. Intended for the storage of blankets and linens, the window seat held a jumble of household stuff. I had recently found some old letters deep inside, and took a few out to show Cathy.

"Look at these," I said.

Written by my mom's brother Jim, the letters held postmarks from California and Hawaii, places so exotic I could hardly imagine them. The word *Aloha* was printed on some of the envelopes, along with a drawing of a palm tree and a hula girl. The letters from Uncle Jim were mostly about fishing and things he could buy cheap in Japan when he went there with the Navy. But there were also letters from his wife, Margaret, and those were more interesting.

I figured out that Margaret was the mother of my cousins, Benny and Jane. Something had happened to her but I didn't know what. Benny and Jane had a stepmother, and no one ever said anything about Margaret, but I had seen pictures of her among our family snapshots, some with her name written on the back. There were pictures of Margaret with Uncle Jim in Hawaii, and some of her with Benny and Jane when they were little.

It seemed strange to think of my cousins living in such an unusual place, with such a beautiful mother. By 1967 Benny had been sent to Vietnam, and Jane was in high school—their childhood ancient history.

Cathy and I were on our knees in front of the window seat when I pointed out the hula girls and the airmail stamps on the letters. "Cool," she said with an indifferent tone. So I tossed the old envelopes aside and we moved on to my mom's closet.

I opened the narrow closet door and shoved all the rarely worn dresses and coats down the rod, revealing shelves where I knew there was a locked metal box. We were looking for the key to this box when Cathy found an old paper bag, soft with age. She opened it and pulled something out.

"What's this?" She handed it to me.

I held a book in my hands—a baby book—with a silky yellow cover and the illustration of an infant sitting under a tree. I knew I held something significant, and felt uneasy about what that might be.

"Open it up," Cathy demanded.

And so I sat on the edge of my mom's bed, opened the baby book, and read a birth announcement taped onto the first page:

Announcing a new arrival!
Baby's name: Hilary Ann
Date: 11-13-54
Weight: 8lbs., 2oz.
Proud parents: Ann Preston

That was *my* name. My birth date.

It all clicked into place for me as my belly flip-flopped and my heart thumped fast. But Cathy looked puzzled. "Who's Ann Preston?" she asked.

I parsed it out slowly. "My cousin's mother's sister."

I explained about how Benny and Jane's real mother had a sister named Ann. I had seen pictures of her, tucked into some of the old letters. I had recently held those pictures and looked at her face—a full, pretty face with a nice smile.

"So, what happened? Did your parents *adopt* you from her?"

"I don't know. I guess." My hands shook as I turned the pages in the baby book. Inside, I found a congratulations card from Aunt Margaret and Uncle Jim, a chart with my height and weight up to six months, and a page filled in with the facts of my birth and my family tree. I was born in San Jose, California. I had a grandmother named Mary Preston and an aunt named Hilary. *Hilary!* But the "Father" side of my tree had been left blank.

I didn't wonder how I ended up in Michigan or why I had never been told any of this. I could only think about the fact that my mom was not my *real* mom, my dad was *not* my dad—a bewildering revelation mixed with a strange delight.

I was someone else, someone with a mysterious past.

"Don't tell anyone," I said.

"I won't."

"Swear."

"I swear. I won't," Cathy said.

I had looked in places I should not have been looking and found things I was not meant to find. I worried my mom would be mad at me for that. And I felt afraid, though I could not have put the fear into words, that this discovery would mean the loss of my mom as my *mom*—that it would alter our bond.

I put the baby book back in the bag and back on the shelf, exactly where it had been. I put it away and tried not to think of it, though of course that wasn't possible. I thought about those pictures I had seen, pictures of Margaret's sister, Ann.

My *mother.*

My *real* mother.

It would take a long time for this astonishing fact to sink in.

CHAPTER 2

Americanized

Almost as soon as I found my mother, I lost her. Within a few months of discovering the baby book, I learned that Ann Preston had been killed in a car accident. But I didn't immediately want to know the details about that accident. I could only absorb so much at once. The desire to know the whole story emerged slowly, and I learned it bit by bit, from a variety of sources, over a period of many years.

As an adult I formed a close relationship with my maternal grandmother, Mary Preston, and the story should really begin with her. Born in the Kensington neighborhood of London, England in 1907, Mary attended a boarding school as a girl and, as a teenager in the 1920s, loved to dance the Charleston.

Mary's father, a physician, wanted her to be a pharmacist, but she preferred going to parties and did not concentrate on her studies as she later wished she would have. In 1927 she married John Beresford Preston, without her family's consent.

John had been a pilot in the Royal Air Force. A charmer with thick wavy hair, he made his living as a salesman of household goods, which I think means he peddled his wares from door to door. His youngest daughter, my aunt Hilary, described him as a charlatan. A con.

"My father was very good at sweet-talking women into buying his merchandise," Aunt Hilary once told me. "He would do anything to support his family—beg, borrow, or steal if necessary."

He would sometimes even sell his own household goods.

"Mum would come home to find the rugs gone!"

Aunt Hilary remembers rooms full of vacuums at one point in her childhood. Another time it was engines, and another it was liquid soap. My grandparents moved frequently in the 1930s. According to my grandmother, they easily moved from one seaside place to another because of the Depression. "You could go wherever you wanted and immediately be given the best accommodations," she said. My mother, Ann, was born in 1931 in a place called Gorleston-On-Sea, a resort town on England's east coast.

I told my grandmother I couldn't imagine moving around so much, especially with so many children—she eventually had eight—but she said she didn't mind. "We often stayed at hotels, so I didn't have the normal chores of running a household. And I was a big believer in sunbathing. My children were all very healthy. We used to live on the beach a lot and I liked them to go as near naked as possible."

The Preston family's nomadic ways came to an end at the beginning of World War II. Called upon to train young pilots for the RAF, my grandfather was stationed at Duxford, an airfield near the university town of Cambridge, for the duration of the war.

My mother's eldest sibling, John Preston Jr., lived with his parents in Cambridge, but the younger siblings—Margaret, Ann,

Christina, Hilary, Billy, and David—were evacuated to the safety of the countryside. In an operation called "Pied Piper," thousands of English parents took their children to railroad stations, not knowing where they would end up. The children were given stamped postcards to send home when they arrived.

Ann was eight years old when the war began in England and fourteen when it ended. I don't know anything about her life during that time, but I have read about the experiences of young English war evacuees. Some were luckier than others, taken into homes where they were well cared for, but many did not fare so well. Being separated from their parents and living with strangers during a time of war had a lasting traumatic impact.

I was not aware that my mother and her siblings had been evacuees until after my grandmother died, so I never discussed the details of this with her. Whenever I asked my grandmother about the war, she always recalled it fondly. She described it as an exciting time with lots of interesting people around and good-looking men in uniform—"lots of handsome Americans." Mary enjoyed telling stories about England and history, but was evasive about her personal history. I'm sure she kept many things to herself, and I'm sorry I didn't pry more persistently.

After the war, the Preston family lived in London, the first time the whole family lived together in many years, which undoubtedly took some adjustment. Casual photographs of the Prestons taken in their garden during this time reveal books, gardening tools, and piles of yarn and knitting needles. Everyone appears to be industriously engaged; everyone *except* my grandmother. She looks thin and grim, her mouth tightly set, her eyes cast away from the camera.

My grandmother once described the first part of her marriage as full of dancing and laughter, and the last part as overwhelmed with difficulties, though she never elaborated on those difficulties. I know she temporarily abandoned her family at one point after the war, and she sometimes referred to my grandfather as mentally ill and erratic, but never gave any details about that. My grandparents divorced in the late 1940s, and my grandfather soon remarried.

What I've been told about the Preston family history is sketchy, but I'm grateful to know it at all, and even more grateful to possess a collection of their photographs. One of my favorite family photos is of Ann, Margaret, and their brother, John, in London. Written on the back of this photo are the words: *This picture was taken at the Lyceum dance hall in the Strand, May 29, 1947.*

The three siblings have big, happy smiles in this photograph. John, wearing his British Navy uniform has a broken tooth and big ears; Margaret, with a soft-looking cardigan on her shoulders, is seventeen and beautiful; and Ann, sixteen, reminds me of myself at that age—the source of my wide cheeks and wavy hair. When I look at this photograph I can almost hear big band music playing. Swinging tunes and sentimental melodies. I imagine my mother dancing with some young sailor or pilot, maybe an American, handsome and heroic.

Margaret Preston met Jim Rutledge, an American Navy man, and married him in January 1948. In their wedding photograph, Margaret and Jim stand on the wide marble steps of the St. Marylebone Registry Office on what looks like a cold, rainy day. Margaret is wearing a winter coat with a corsage and a little white hat, while her groom stands with his hand awkwardly at her elbow. Transferred to the United States within a year of their wedding, Jim and Margaret were eventually stationed in California and Hawaii.

My mother, Ann, worked in a nursery school in the late 1940s, and then for an American military family as their nanny. In September of 1950, at the age of nineteen, she traveled to the United States on an ocean liner with this family. She lived first in Washington, D.C., then in a small town near Philadelphia. She must have lived in these places with the family she worked for, but all I know for sure is what I've learned from her passport and from letters she wrote to her youngest sister, Hilary. In a letter from Philadelphia postmarked February 1951, she wrote:

> Dear Hill,
>
> How come I never hear from you? Sure would like to know how you are getting on. How do you like working in a nursery? I was so pleased to hear you had started and hope you go right through with your training. Don't be like your two foolish sisters, you stick to it. And don't accept any offers to come to the States as I did, as I don't think you would be happy.
>
> Life can get awful lonesome in a strange country and a small town where you don't know anybody. Although I will never regret my trip over here or the fine time I had in Washington, all good things have to come to an end and you have to settle down to hard work.
>
> I can't grumble really as I've had a chance to visit with Margaret. I have also met a nice English family living here

and go round and see them quite a bit, but frankly except for Margie being here I am quite ready to go back to dear old England. After all there is no place like home. [...]

Ann eventually came to live with Margaret in Alameda, California, for about a year, and then on her own in San Francisco. In a picture taken in March of 1953, Ann has transformed into a well-dressed woman. Posed outdoors next to some foliage, she looks stylish and chic. Her hair has been lightened, and she's wearing a jacket with puffy sleeves.

Jim Rutledge once said he thought my mother was a nice English girl who got "Americanized," but I'm not sure what he meant by this. I can only imagine what it would have been like to live in sunny 1950s California after growing up during the war and in postwar London. From grey austerity to Technicolor.

Sometime in 1953, my mother moved to Las Vegas. I don't know what prompted her move, but I know she met my father there, and she must have worked in a casino. The Clark County Sheriff's Office issued an identification card to Ann Preston on August 31, 1953. A necessity for Las Vegas casino employees, this identification card has her signature on the front and the fingerprints of her right hand on the back.

Her fingerprints.

I have pressed my fingers up against these ink images, the unique whorls and lines and shape of my mother's fingers—much smaller than mine. It's as close as I come to her physical being, to physical evidence of her existence. I have to remind myself that she was real, really *my* mother, and not just a character in this story I have come to know.

There is only one photograph of my mother in Las Vegas. An eight-by-ten, it was taken from outside, looking through a big rectangular window. A sign inside the window says, *Station KORK presents "Midnite along Fremont St." with Jack Kogan.* There is a record player, a microphone, and a display of various items in the window, including a ventriloquist's dummy and an advertisement for De Soto full-power steering.

Jack Kogan, a well-known Las Vegas broadcasting personality, sits in front of the microphone, and my mother stands next to him, turned sideways and smiling. I'm sure it delighted her to interact with a local celebrity, and he was most likely charmed by her English accent.

I treasure this photograph, but it elicits unanswered questions. Did my mother pose with Jack Kogan the way a tourist would, or was the photo set up as some kind of publicity shot? Did my mother work at the place where the photo was taken? Or was she there specifically because of Kogan, or the photographer? Did she know the photographer?

That's the thing I wonder about the most: who took this picture? Who went outside to look into the window, take the photo, have it developed into an eight-by-ten print, and then give it to my mother?

For many years I wondered if my father took this photograph. And I romantically imagined that to be so. I imagined the moment the shutter clicked and *saw* my father—a tall, dark-eyed Air Force officer, a handsome guy with a camera. My father is listed on my birth certificate as "unknown." But a paragraph in a letter written by Margaret Preston led me to believe he had been an officer in the military.

> [...] I do think it was unfair of that fellow (the father) not to have at least offered to help her out. All she asked of him was for enough money to leave Las Vegas and to live on for a few days and he gave her $20! I don't know how far he thought $20 could go—and an officer, too!

If the accident hadn't happened, I assume my mother would have told me something about my father someday. I assume she would have told me *something*. And I wonder what that would have been.

CHAPTER 3

The Las Vegas Story

"Where are my ancestors from?"

My twin sons were in middle school when one of them asked me this question. They had recently added the word *ancestor* to their vocabulary, but I didn't have much of an answer for them. Divorced from their dad, I knew little about my sons' paternal lineage, and only half of my own family history.

Up to that point in my life I had rarely wondered about the identity of my biological father. I thought of him the way you would an abstract concept. I knew my brown eyes must have come from him, since all my Preston relatives had blue eyes, but no one knew his name.

The letter from Margaret, in which she says my father had been an officer, was my only solid clue, and I presumed he had been in the Air Force because there is a base in Las Vegas. I told my sons their grandfather had likely been an Air Force officer.

"A guy who flew jet planes?"

Justin and Jeremy, my tall, blond sons, loved the idea of being descendant from a fighter jet pilot, and I loved giving them an ancestor they could idealize. "Yes," I told them. *Yes*. A guy who flew jet planes. And with that, an image of my father took shape. He began to seem like an actual person to me for the first time, a person I would like to know.

I decided to do some investigating, in spite of my lack of clues. And since I didn't yet own a computer, I began by sending letters to places like the hospital where I was born and Air Force retiree groups. I did what I could for a couple of years, got nowhere, and gave up. I declared the search for my father impossible. But my curiosity had been aroused and would no longer rest. It felt like someone tapping me on the shoulder, persistently trying to get my attention, until finally, in the spring of 2006, I decided to search again, this time with the internet at my fingertips.

My sons were grown and on their own by then, and my personal life had settled down after a long period of tumult and transition. While married to my second husband, I had a romantic relationship with a woman. I came out in 1999, the year my sons graduated from high school, and subsequently changed nearly everything about my life. By 2006 I was living with my partner Beth. When I told her I wanted to search for my father and write about the experience as I went along, she said that sounded like a good idea.

And so I began, unprepared for how difficult the search would be, or how obsessively it would consume me. On March 10, 2006, I opened a file drawer in my home office and took out a fat green folder labeled *Father Search*. I hadn't opened this folder for several years, and one of the first things I found inside it was a letter I wrote to the Oprah Winfrey Show—never sent—asking for help. I had written this letter in response to one of Oprah's reunion shows. Tear-jerking episodes that featured biological parents reuniting with their adult children, in front of a studio audience.

I only got halfway through my old letter to Oprah before I crumpled it up and threw it away, embarrassed by my naiveté. I might as well have been writing to Santa. Even if Oprah had picked my plea from the thousands she must have received, how could she have helped without a name or any kind of document to go on? My parents had never legally adopted me, so there was no paper trail to follow.

I closed my old file folder, pushed it aside, and typed "Las Vegas 1950s history" into my computer. This led to a site of vintage postcard images. I clicked on a postcard of Fremont Street and there it was: the place where my mother had most likely met my father. Fremont Street was still the heart of Las Vegas in the early 1950s. It hadn't yet been overshadowed by Las Vegas Boulevard, the magnificent "strip." Las Vegas was young and new when my mother lived there, the Sands and the Sahara had just opened for business in 1952.

I studied the images of old Las Vegas and imagined my mother in the places they depicted. The windows of the El Cortez resembled those in the picture of my mother with Jack Kogan. But then I inspected the Horseshoe casino and saw that its windows were also similar.

I wondered why I had never researched old Las Vegas or contacted the radio station, KORK, to ask where Jack Kogan broadcasted from in 1954. *What had I been waiting for?* I began to make a list of things to do. *#1. Contact KORK re. Kogan*, I wrote, then returned to the computer images. I explored the Las Vegas historical sites for a long time, charmed by the iconic images of its golden era: glamorous, sexy, prosperous, and exciting.

I found myself becoming fascinated by Las Vegas, although it had never appealed to me before. My perceptions of Vegas had formed during my teenage years, the 1970s. I associated it with people in polyester leisure suits. With fat Elvis in sequins. And that image stuck with me. But suddenly I wanted to know all about it. I logged on to Amazon and ordered a book about Las Vegas history. I also ordered a CD called *Jackpot! The Las Vegas Story*, featuring songs by Vic Damone, Mel Tormé, and Wayne Newton.

In the summer of 1962 my mom and two aunts took me and a cousin on a trip to Disneyland. We drove from Michigan to California in a station wagon and stopped in Las Vegas along the way. I was only seven, so I have few memories of that trip, but I do remember staying at the Blue Angel Motel in Las Vegas. I remember the big, blue angel on the roof, and I remember the sidewalk: so hot you couldn't walk barefoot on it.

Unfortunately, there aren't any pictures of our visit to Vegas except for some we took in a photo booth at Woolworth's. Frequently found in "dime stores" in those days, photo booths produced strips of four photos that developed in a few minutes.

While sitting next to my mom in the photo booth that hot day in Las Vegas, the camera snapped while she was in the middle of saying something, so two of the pictures came out looking like she was about to throw up.

When my mom and aunts saw these pictures, they laughed so hard they practically peed their pants, right there in the middle of the store. They were doubling over, clutching their sides and pulling tissues out of their purses to dab at their watering eyes. But I didn't see the humor. Their behavior mortified me, and I thought the picture strip was *awful* – though now I'm glad to have it.

The first shot would be a good one, except for the sunglasses I'm holding at a jaunty angle, obscuring part of my face. I'm a cute kid in these photos, my hair in a pixie cut. I'm hamming it up in the next two shots, the ones in which my mom looks sick. But the fourth photo on the strip is fine. Marie is smiling, her arm around me. We're close together, me and my mom, my *everything* – comfort, security, best friend. We're together on vacation having fun, and everything is just as it should be. I love her completely and I am completely loved in return

CHAPTER 4

The Happiest Girl in the World

My mom, Marie Rutledge, grew up in Trenton, Michigan, the last town along the Detroit River before it flows into Lake Erie. Her family lived in a small, one-story house in Trenton and just managed to get by during the Depression. Thrifty and practical, the Rutledge family grew a large garden, put up canned goods, and wore clothes that were sewn at home.

Marie's brothers, Jim and Tom, both joined the Navy as soon as they could, and Marie took a job in a factory. She dropped out of high school in the eleventh grade to take advantage of wartime opportunities for women. Hired by Firestone, which had been given a defense contract to make rubberized military products, she went to work each day with a lunch pail in her hand and her hair tied up in a kerchief. Like the iconic Rosie the Riveter, Marie gladly did her part for the war effort and gladly collected her pay. A hardworking gal, just five foot two, Marie most often wore slacks, but there are photos of her in the 1940s wearing fashionable hats, high heels, and a big fur coat.

In 1943, at the age of nineteen, Marie married Sylvester Bocianowski. Syl was a steelworker, a Polish immigrant ten years her elder. "I liked his blue eyes," she said when explaining why she fell for him, but I have trouble imagining this. I can't picture the people I knew as my parents as young and in love.

The Navy trained Marie's brother, Jim Rutledge, to be an airplane mechanic. After the end of World War II, while stationed in England, he met Margaret Preston, a seventeen-year-old beauty. They met at a baseball game in Hyde Park.

Jim and Margaret were married in London in January of 1948, and later that year Margaret flew to the United States. While Jim took part in the Berlin Airlift, Margaret stayed with the Rutledges in their drab little house in Trenton, pregnant with my cousin Benny. Margaret lived with her in-laws for several months, and I can't imagine what she did all day, or what she talked to Jim's quiet, dull mother about. The company of Jim's sister, Marie, must have been a welcome distraction. And later, while living in California and Hawaii, Margaret kept up a correspondence with her sister-in-law.

On June 10, 1954, Margaret wrote to Marie from Hawaii:

> [...] As I told you in my last letter we are leaving here in August, just when in August we don't know for sure, and we still don't know where we're going, but I'm pretty sure we are going back to California.
>
> I honestly don't see how we can raise the money to make the trip to see you Marie, we don't have a cent in

the bank, but I'm sure we will be able to make the trip next year. I've got to start a bank account, also get that money we owe to your mother paid off, and the kids will need a lot of new clothes to start school in.

My sister is in trouble. She is having a baby and needs help. We are going to take care of her, and in exchange she is going to take care of the kids so that I can go to work. I don't know if she intends to keep the baby. If I didn't have any children, I would adopt it.

If we had the money in the bank I would have sent her the money to come here. She is in San Francisco now and very unhappy and alone. The Red Cross is helping her until we get there.

Goodness, so far all I have written about is money, let's change the subject. Jimmy has gone on another trip. He goes on so many I don't even have time to ask him where he is going anymore. Since they got the new planes they are not gone half as long as they used to. It used to take them almost 10 days to go to Japan, now they are only gone 4 days.

I took the kids to see *Go Man Go* this evening. It only cost 35 cents to go to a movie on the base. We go about once a week. Have you seen any 3D pictures? We saw *The House of Wax* and enjoyed it very much. I am now an American citizen, thank goodness. The examination was real easy. Write again soon.

Love,
Margaret, Jimmy, and the kids

Margaret must have been disenchanted with life as a Navy wife by this time. Tired of not having enough money, she couldn't have looked forward to having her sister's baby to worry about. So in a letter to her childless sister-in-law she suggests, "If I didn't have any children, I would adopt it."

Dear Marie,

I have just come from the commissary and found your letter of the 15th in the mail box. About Ann's baby, I guess I shouldn't have mentioned it. She's already nuts about that baby. I think she intends to keep it, but I will write and tell her that you would like to adopt it. She is living with a family in San Francisco now, and they are taking care of her.

Marie, if Ann decides to let you adopt the baby, you will have to arrange to be there when it's born. I'm sure that if she sees it she will change her mind. She won't need hospital fees, but I'm sure she would like some money to make a fresh start. Anyway, the decision is up to Ann herself.

We only have about eight more weeks to go in Hawaii and then we will be heading back to the states. Jimmy left for Travis Air Force Base in California last night. I sure wish I could go with him, I want to see Ann so much. I know she has changed for the better since all this happened. [...]

I'm not sure what Margaret means when she says that Ann has "changed for the better since all this happened." I don't know if she means this sincerely or if it's just for Marie's benefit, a way to assure her that Ann is repentant, a good girl who made a mistake, and not a tramp. She says "the decision is up to Ann herself" but mentions that some money would be nice.

Dear Marie and Syl,

I have the most wonderful news for you. You are going to become parents in October! Ann is willing to let you adopt her baby. I have just received a letter from her saying she is happy you suggested it, she wants it to go to someone she knows so that she will know how it is getting along. But you will have to have it all done legally Marie. I don't know how one goes about adopting a baby so you had better see a lawyer.

Another thing Marie, you will have to arrange to pick the baby up at the hospital as soon as it is born. One good thing about all this is we will get to see you when you get here, and I hope you will stay with us for a few days.

I'm so happy for you, Marie and Syl. I know Ann will have a pretty baby and I think she will have a son, as she is having all the same symptoms I had with Benny. You had better get your spare room fixed up in blue!

Jimmy just came home for lunch and we discussed the idea of you adopting the baby. He said he doesn't think there is any legal way to adopt a baby except through an agency, and a lawyer would cost a fortune, so I don't know what to think.

Maybe Ann will agree to let it go without signing anything, but it would be a lot safer if there were some sort of documents signed, don't you think? Anyway, it will have to be between you and Ann whatever you decide to do. The best of luck.

Love,
Margaret

On the back of this letter is a note from Marie written in pencil. "Syl, this makes me the happiest girl in the world. I don't care how much it costs, we're going to have a son! Love, Marie. P.S. If your soup is rotten please don't blame me. I don't know what I'm doing since I got this letter."

Dear Marie,

Many thanks for your letter of the 30th, I just received it today. I'm going to be chewing my nails until that baby is safely in Michigan!

We should know by the end of this month where we are going, but regardless of where, we will take Ann with us, she needs a family. She cried just talking to Benny on the phone the other day.

I know I am going to see a much changed Ann. I do think it was unfair of that fellow (the father) not to have at least offered to help her out. All she asked of him was for enough money to leave Las Vegas and to live on for a few days and he gave her $20! I don't know how far he thought $20 could go, and an officer, too!

How sad about Marcella's husband drowning. I hope this will scare Syl into learning to swim. I would be worried sick if Jimmy went fishing as much as Syl does and couldn't swim! How is Syl by the way? Still as crazy as ever? (Only kidding of-course.)

We are going to try and rent a house outside of Navy housing when we leave here. The houses that the Navy provides are so small and there is no privacy, as there are so many families crowded together. We might have to sell the car to do it, but it will be worth it.

What is the baby furniture you have picked out like? I just got rid of Jane's crib, or you could have had it. I still have that nice blue stroller that I got in London, but I think I'll keep it in case we have another baby.

Well Marie, I had better stop and fix lunch.

Love,
Margaret and Jimmy

P.S. What are you going to name the baby?

I don't remember when I first discovered these letters. My mom repeatedly told me to stay out of the window seat in her room because my dad's hunting rifle and ammunition were stored there, but I couldn't resist. The creak of the lid always gave me a little thrill.

I occasionally had the house to myself on weekend afternoons when my mom went to the grocery store or a union meeting, and my dad was at work, or the bar, or fishing. That's when I would snoop around, and maybe try on some of my mom's old clothes. I enjoyed playing dress-up long after I had exceeded the age when it is considered a cute thing to do, though I would have died of embarrassment if anyone knew.

There were old purses inside the window seat, some with matchbooks, tubes of lipstick, coins, and costume jewelry still in them. Artifacts of a long gone era, it seemed odd to me that these stylish things once belonged to my mom. I hardly ever saw her wear anything but her work clothes or her pajamas.

The letters from Margaret were at the bottom of the window seat, along with a lot of other junk: postcards, brochures, maps, magazines, and things like that. There were also letters from Jim Rutledge and my grandmother, scattered here and there. I didn't read the letters all the way through when I found them. I only read snippets, quickly, always afraid I would be caught.

I had no idea these letters had anything to do with me; they were simply fascinating relics of the past. I loved the thin paper and matching envelopes, the postmarks, the handwriting. And I loved that you could open these letters and know what people said to each other so long ago, though most of the snippets I read were mundane.

One afternoon, while wearing red lipstick and my mom's fur coat, I took a few of the letters out of the window seat. I took them to my bedroom, stashed them in an old Barbie case, and shoved it under my dresser.

I don't remember why I did this, mostly just curiosity, I think. Nosiness. Though I also, somehow, must have sensed the letters' significance.

July 23, 1954

Dear Marie and Syl,

Many thanks for your letter received today. I got a letter from Ann yesterday, but she didn't mention the baby. I told her I was sick of hearing about it. She wrote and broke the news to my mother the other day. I only hope Mother doesn't try to talk Ann into keeping the baby.

We got word that we are going to San Jose, California for next duty. San Jose is a very lovely part of California, about 50 miles from San Francisco. We will be near the university and Palo Alto valley. I'm dying to get there and get settled. We are going to be pretty busy from now till Christmas. I guess you and Syl will have a very happy Christmas this year!

I told Ann to start looking around for an apartment, as we will need a place to stay for a few weeks until we find a house in San Jose. I have got a lot of the packing done already. All I have left to pack are our clothes.

I wish someone would talk Jimmy into getting some new clothes. He ruined all his shirts and pants by working on cars. He wouldn't dream of wearing overalls, he has to ruin his good clothes! If it wasn't for the Navy I think he would go around in rags! He just doesn't care what he looks like. Maybe when you see him you could casually ask him when he is going to get himself his first suit. It's his birthday August 25th. [...]

Love,
Margaret

I have two letters that my mother, Ann, wrote to my mom, Marie. I found these in the window seat along with all the others, though I don't remember when. It took a while to find all the letters, sneaking them out a few at a time. The first letter from Ann is postmarked July 1954, from San Francisco.

Dear Marie,

Thank you so much for both your letters. [...] I don't quite know how to put this, but I have been wondering and wondering if I have done the right thing in saying you can have my baby. Not that I don't want you to have it if I let it go, but I am afraid that I am going to want to keep it myself.

I know how much you want a child. But this is my baby, I am going to give birth to it, and I am afraid I may change my mind at the last minute, and that wouldn't be fair to you.

At first when Margaret told me about you I thought it might be a good idea, but I told her not to tell you as I wanted to think about it a little before doing anything I would be sorry for.

Then I got your letter saying how you were looking at baby furniture and how thrilled you were, so I thought of all the things you could give the baby that I wouldn't be able to right now. And as Margaret had already told you I was going to let you have the baby I honestly thought that might be the best thing. But now I am going to have to ask you to wait.

I realize how you are going to feel and I have thought about this a great deal. I couldn't sleep last night for thinking about it. Here the baby is kicking around like mad inside me and I wonder if I'm doing the right thing?

It's not going to be easy for me with a baby, I know. But I have met so many nice, kind people who want to help. I was desperate when I first came here from Las Vegas. I had no idea what I was going to do or how I would manage, but I have got along so far. Once I get on my feet I can get a job. Lots of girls have done it and I am sure I could, too.

I was sick and confused when I got your letter. All I could think of was getting this over with, starting again, and forgetting it ever happened. But could I forget? There is still the child, and I would always wonder about it. Knowing where it was might not help.

Please, please Marie, try and understand. If you were me what would you do? I don't think you would give your child up!

The baby is due around the 16th of November, so that still gives us some time. I do hope you haven't gone ahead and got a lot of things for the baby. That's why I'm writing. Just wait awhile. It's not fair to you to have everything ready and then be disappointed. [...] Please understand and be patient. I am just doing what I think is best.

All the best always,
Ann

I've read this letter so many times now, I practically know it by heart. Certain sentences resonate in my mind like lines of poetry: *wondering and wondering if I have done the right thing…here the baby is kicking around like mad inside me…* How miraculous it seems to me to read my mother's words, almost like hearing her voice, saved on these few thin sheets of paper.

July 28, 1954

Dear Marie and Syl,

I just don't know how to say how terribly sorry I was to hear that Ann had changed her mind about the baby, but there is nothing stronger than mother love and it is the most important thing for a baby.

Marie, can't you try and adopt a baby from an agency, or maybe your doctor knows of a girl who is having a baby and wants it adopted, quite a lot of people get babies this way, in fact that's what I suggested to Ann when she wrote and told me she was in trouble.

We have more or less decided to buy a house in Sunnyvale. It only costs $185 for the down-payment and then $61.50 a month. That is cheaper than renting a house. I do hope this doesn't change your mind about coming to stay with us. I'm so looking forward to seeing you.

We are just sitting around and waiting to leave here. I'm all packed up and ready to go. I do hope Ann will change her mind.

Love and XXX from us both,
Margaret and Jimmy

The second letter from Ann to Marie is dated August 10, 1954.

Dear Marie,

I expect you have been hoping for an answer to your letter. I hate to think of you being so upset, but I just can't see handing the baby over to someone else even if it will be hard for me to try and raise it myself. I just wish that you had never thought there was a chance for you to have the child, especially when you want a baby so badly.

Yes, the agency will help me before and after the baby comes. No, I don't have to pay the agency back, they are there to help anybody who needs help. I am sure I will be able to manage, and I would only be miserable giving the baby up. I just haven't the heart to do it.

While I write this Margaret and the children should be flying over the Pacific on their way to San Francisco. They should be here tonight. I can't wait to see them and decide what we will do about living together.

I was sorry to hear that you won't be coming for a visit. I feel like I have spoiled all your plans. I just don't know what to say except that I hope you will try and understand and not think badly about me for disappointing you this way.

God bless you Marie.
Always,
Ann

CHAPTER 5

Photographs

My cousin Jane had just turned five when the accident that killed our mothers happened. She doesn't remember anything about Margaret. While growing up, Jane knew her mother had come from England and that she'd been killed in a car accident, but little more than that. Her dad and her stepmother didn't talk about the past, and there were no photos of Margaret on display in their home.

The trauma of losing a parent at such a young age must have been compounded by having that parent essentially erased, but Jane never feels sorry for herself. "I guess you can't miss what you never really had," she says. Yet she speaks about her mother often when we're together.

Fit and trim, with a sunny personality and eyes so light they're nearly invisible, Jane married at eighteen and divorced in her late forties. She runs a dog-grooming business out of her home, drove a school bus for many years, and participates in country line-dancing twice a week. We see each other infrequently, and long stretches of time go by between phone calls, but we are bonded by our history and our loss.

The only pictures Jane and I had of our mothers for many years were a handful of snapshots. But then Jane made a surprising discovery. While cleaning out her father's attic after his death in 1987, Jane found several photo albums she had never seen before, including two that had been Margaret's, and one, which I didn't realize until many years later, had been Ann's.

Packed in a cardboard box for more than thirty years, these large rectangular albums held hundreds of photographs which made our mothers' lives more tangible to us. Here they were as girls and young women in London. Here were their family and friends, their hairstyles, clothes, and happy moments. And then here they were, in California, with us.

It shocked me to learn these treasures had never been shown to Jane and Benny.

Jane traveled across Michigan to share the photo albums with me soon after she found them. We spent a long afternoon at my dining room table studying the photos in detail, and while we were at it I pulled some pictures of my mother out of the little black corner tabs that held them in place. I didn't ask Jane's permission to do this for fear she'd say no. I just took what I wanted as fast as I could.

Considering how rarely I spend time with Jane, I didn't know when I would have the chance to look at these albums again. Even though I'm sure she would have let me have a few photos if I had asked, I couldn't chance it. I couldn't wait. I had to have the photo of my mother with me in her arms. I had to have one of her with her sisters, one of her with her mother, and the 8 X 10 of her and Jack Kogan.

In one of the pictures I acquired that day, my mother is posed in Jim and Margaret's backyard in California. She is dressed in her best, seated on a lawn chair, her face in profile. I removed this picture from the album, but didn't notice until later that my mother had written on the back of it: *To Stanley, with all my love, your Ann.*

She wrote this and then crossed it out. It looks like she wanted to have a nice picture to give this Stanley guy but changed her mind, or selected another shot. And when I saw what my mother wrote, I became convinced this photo had been intended for my father. *Stanley.* I felt certain about this, and searched only for men with that name during my first search efforts—a regrettable mistake. Several years later, when I finally had the chance to look at the photo albums again, I noticed the picture inscribed to Stanley had been on a page labeled "1952," two years before my birth.

When I began to search again, in 2006, I started from scratch. I knew my father had been a military officer, and I felt certain he had been stationed near Las Vegas when he met my mother. They knew each other long enough for her to confirm her pregnancy and ask him for help leaving town. And in those days, before at-home pregnancy tests, that had to have been at least two months.

I devised a plan in which I would obtain rosters of all the officers stationed at bases near Las Vegas at the time of my conception, and then investigate those names. I learned I could file Freedom of Information Act (FOIA) requests for these kinds of records and quickly became enthused about being a sleuth. I made a list of all the leads I could follow and came up with ten things:

1. Contact KORK re. Kogan photo
2. FOIA request Nellis
3. FOIA request Fallon
4. Clark County: Las Vegas ID card
5. Sunnyvale Medical Center records
6. San Francisco Red Cross
7. John and Betty Bias
8. The Valverdes
9. John Wales
10. The woman in *People* magazine

Nellis is the Air Force base in Las Vegas; Fallon is a Naval Air Station in Nevada; John and Betty Bias were friends with Jim and Margaret; the Valverdes lived next door when I was born; John Wales was the sailor driving the car on the night of the accident; and the woman in *People* magazine is a stranger who looked remarkably like me.

Once I started thinking about pursuing these leads, it was *all* I could think about. I became preoccupied. Hopeful. And I began keeping a journal of my progress—the catalyst that led to the writing of this book. In one of my first journal entries I wrote about finding Betty Bias.

Search Journal: March 13, 2006

There are several photos in Margaret's photo albums of a couple named John and Betty Bias, including one in which they are sitting on a sofa with my mother in Sunnyvale. Their name is written on the back of this photo: *John and Betty Bias 1950.*

I have wondered about this couple for a long time and finally Googled them this morning. When I typed their name into my computer, up popped the genealogy site of their daughter, Sharon. From there I learned that John Bias died in 1989, but Betty is still living in California.

I sent an e-mail to Sharon asking if her mother remembered Jim and Margaret and if she would be interested in talking to me about them. I thought I might hear from her in a few days or so, but got a reply this afternoon.

> Hi, I know the name of the Rutledges very well. Their name often came up in discussions my parents had about their life in England. My mother, although almost homebound due to arthritis, is still sharp as a tack. She can probably remember everything about that time. I'm sure she'd enjoy a call.

I exchanged several more e-mails with Sharon and made plans to talk to her mother tomorrow. But now I'm full of nervous anxiety. *What will I say to this woman?*

March 14, 2006

I felt uneasy all day about talking to Betty Bias, though I'm not sure why. I'd chalk it up to a kind of stage fright, but it was more than that, a fear of the unknown perhaps, or maybe a fear of asking questions that deep down I still feel guilty for asking. I still sometimes feel like a nosy kid, snooping into places where I'm not supposed to be.

I put off dialing as long as I could, but when I finally made the call my fears were eased by Betty's cheerful tone. She said she was glad to hear from me. I told her I had been looking at a lot of old pictures. "I'd like to know about the time when you knew Jim and Margaret Rutledge. I'm wondering if you could share your memories with me."

"Well, I'd be happy to," she said.

Betty told me that Jim and her husband were buddies in the Navy and rented a house together in London when they were stationed there. "You had to find your own housing," she explained. Jim was a mechanic and John Bias was a radio operator. "They took planes all over the world."

The Navy sent Betty to be with her husband in England in 1947. They rented their own apartment when she arrived but spent a lot of time with Jim and Margaret. "We were always all together," she said. "We liked to go play baseball in Hyde Park. The whole group of us used to meet down there."

Several years later the Biases and the Rutledges lived near each other in California and stayed in touch. She told me about a driving tour they took of all the missions in California, starting from San Diego and working their way up the coast. "Oh, we had good times. We played cards a lot, went on picnics to Golden Gate Park, and the fellows went on fishing trips."

I asked Betty about my mother, and she told me Ann had lived in San Francisco for a while and then went to Las Vegas.

I asked if she knew what made my mother go to Las Vegas, and she said she didn't know. I asked if she knew what kind of work my mother did in San Francisco, and she didn't know that either. I then asked if she knew anything about my father and she said, "Not a word."

Disappointed, I quickly changed the subject.

"So, do you think Margaret was happy in the States?"

Betty talked about how Margaret and Ann loved the San Francisco area because there was so much to do. "Shows, parks, restaurants...they loved that sort of thing."

Betty asked about my cousins, Benny and Jane. She said what a delight Benny had been as a little boy and how hard it must have been on him to lose his mother at such a young age.

I asked her about the car accident, and she said she didn't know any details about it. "I was just shocked," she said, "so shocked." She expressed her surprise about Jim marrying "the new girl," his second wife, Carol, so soon. "I think he just wanted to have a mother for the children."

Betty told me some more about herself and asked about my life. She remembered me as a round, chubby baby. She said she was glad I called. "I've always wondered what happened to you."

I enjoyed talking to Betty, but hung up feeling discouraged because she didn't know anything about my father. I had been hoping she might have heard his name, or anything at all about him, in gossip from Margaret. I put the receiver down and wondered if I should have pushed her harder about it.

I sat motionless at my desk for a long while after that call, haunted by images the conversation brought to mind, images of carefree days: card games, picnics, shows, parks, restaurants. I sat looking out the window, at bare, winter trees, as a wave of sorrow unexpectedly swelled and broke within me, a deep wave of sorrow for all the things that could have been.

CHAPTER 6

Two Sunnyvale Sisters

Sunnyvale, California
September 8, 1954
Dear Marie,

I got five letters and a cheque today! One of the letters was from you, thanks a lot. Marie dear, please try and be understanding about the baby, it would just about kill Ann to give up that baby now. We have already bought the crib and knitted sweaters and booties.

Ann is living with us and paying $10 a week for rent, and she helps out with the kids a lot. I sure hope you will change your mind and come and visit us, we are buying a new house next month and will have plenty of room, how about it?

It is good to be back in California. Jimmy can't wait to get here, he is due this Saturday. [...] My mother, kid sister, and brother are coming over to the States at the end of next year. You may have a letter from my mother, she wants to get to know you.

Love,
Margaret

Originally famous for its bountiful orchards, Sunnyvale is located southeast of San Francisco, in the area now known as Silicon Valley. The semiconductor chip began transforming the rural village of Sunnyvale into a high-tech city in the 1950s, a time when houses were built in abundance.

September 17, 1954
Dear Marie,

Many thanks for your letter, also the nice birthday card. Jimmy gave me a Bulova bracelet watch for my birthday gift. I gave him socks and shirts. [...] Ann has her baby in about 6 weeks' time. We move into our new house in about 3 weeks [...] Jimmy and I are going to visit your brother Tom this weekend.

October 10, 1954
Dear Marie,

[...] Tom and Alice seem to be happy together, although they are very strict with the kids, especially

Tom, he did nothing but yell at them the whole time we were there.

We hope to be out of this apartment and into our new house very soon. Benny just loves school. His teacher is "Miss Smith" and he still has a lisp so you can imagine him saying it. We haven't been to a show in 6 weeks, but tomorrow we are going to see "Rear Window." It should be good.

Love,
Margaret and Jim

That's the last letter from Margaret until six months later. She may have been too busy getting settled into her new house to write, or all of her letters might not have been saved, but in either case I think it's odd that there isn't a letter telling of my birth.

The one-story tract home that Jim and Margaret bought in Sunnyvale featured a big window in front and a carport attached at the side. Margaret sent a few photos of the house to Marie and put several more into a photo album. In one picture, Benny and Jane are posed at the end of the driveway in a classic baby-boom image: there's the new house, the driveway, and two kids, but no trees or shrubbery yet.

The photos of the tidy kitchen reveal a Formica table, plastic-backed metal chairs, and white metal cabinets. A shot of the living room features a chair with a Hawaiian-themed slipcover, blond end tables, and ceramic knickknacks.

These pictures are all dated December 1954. In one of them, Ann and Margaret stand together in front of the carport. Looking off to the right and smiling, my mother looks pretty good for having recently given birth. At the bottom of this photo, Jim has written, *Last picture together.*

Margaret's last roll of photographs, taken in March of 1955, includes the picture I cherish the most. My mother is standing outside the house in Sunnyvale with me in her arms. She holds me facing outward, her arm across my chest in a loving embrace, her cheek close to mine, and a wide, happy smile on her face.

680 Borregas Avenue
Sunnyvale, California
April 1, 1955
Dear Marie,

Just a few lines to thank you for the nice birthday cards for the kids, and the money. Jimmy left for a month in dear old Honolulu this morning. I would like to have gone with him, a month would be a nice holiday.

Are you still working hard Marie? Do you still have the same job? Ann has a new job in a dress shop, and she does a little modeling too. I think I have a cocktail waitress job in a new place that is opening up near here. It is a very smart place. [...]

Love,
Margaret

P.S. Got sworn in as an American citizen and have been celebrating ever since.

On the last page of Margaret's photo albums there are three pictures. They are small, two and a half inches square, and they have faded to a nearly sepia tint. *The Bonton* is written in the margin of one, which I assume was the name of a restaurant or bar. It might be the "very smart place" Margaret mentioned in her letter.

May 1955 is scrawled across the top of another little picture. My mother stands at the center of it, posed as if she's about to cut a cake, though the cake itself isn't in the shot. A sailor standing at her side has his hand over hers on the knife, as if they are a bride and groom.

My mother's birthday was in May, so I suspect this is her birthday celebration and the sailor is joking around. The picture is a double exposure—a second photo shot on top of the first without the film advancing in the camera. There is the ghost of a smiling woman, a handsome man in a suit, and some sailors floating in the background, giving the photo an artistic look.

The car crash that killed Ann and Margaret happened on June 23 at 12:45 a.m. on Bayshore Highway and Lawrence Road, just a few miles from their home. The driver, a sailor named John Wales, survived. My mother's death certificate states that she was thrown from the vehicle. Her cause of death is listed as "Multiple cervical fractures and ruptured left subclavian vein with extensive facial, neck, mediastinal and retroperitoneal hemorrhage."

At the time of the crash, Jim Rutledge was at home, waiting up. And the next day, when Jim went to the site of the accident, he found Margaret's watch—her brand-new Bulova bracelet watch—in the dirt at the side of the road.

An article appeared in the *San Jose Mercury News* on Friday, June 24, 1955, on page 1.

Two Sunnyvale Sisters Die in Collision

Two Sunnyvale sisters—both natives of England—died in the head-on collision of a car and a giant milk truck on

Bayshore Highway near Lawrence Road in the Sunnyvale area yesterday.

They were Mrs. Margaret Rutledge, 25, of 680 Borregas Ave., Sunnyvale, and Miss Ann Preston, 24, of the same address. Both were in the car. Its third occupant, John Wales, 21, a Moffett Field sailor, received critical injuries.

All three victims were thrown clear of the car after its collision with the milk tanker. Highway Patrolmen yesterday had not established which of the three was driving.

Wales, an aviation electronics technician, was taken to Oak Knoll Hospital at Oakland after being treated at the Moffett Field dispensary. Patrolmen hope to get a statement from him today.

The truck, southbound at the time of the mishap, was driven by Albert Virchow, 40, of Daly City. After the collision it swung around and struck a car driven by Harry M. Gee, 42, a San Francisco cook. Gee and Virchow were not hurt.

Both Mrs. Rutledge and Miss Preston had lived in this country about two years. They leave two sisters and four brothers in England. Mrs. Rutledge is survived by her husband, James, a Navy sailor; a son, Benny; and a daughter, Jane.

Joint funeral services will be held Friday at 3 p.m. at Chapel of the Psalms in Willow Glen. Interments will be in Santa Clara Mission Cemetery.

This article inaccurately states that Ann and Margaret had been in the country "about two years"—information that most likely came from Jim while he was still in shock. It also doesn't mention my existence.

After the accident, Jim returned to Hawaii with Benny and Jane, who were temporarily cared for by a foster mother. A newspaper clipping from the *Honolulu Star-Bulletin* dated Thursday, August 4, 1955, shows a picture of them with this woman. The caption reads:

> Navy man James A. Rutledge smiles happily as he acquaints his two motherless children with Mrs. Mae Tougher of Lanikai. The widow will care for Jane Marie, 5, and Benny James, 6, while Rutledge is on duty. Their mother was killed in an automobile accident on June 23. Determined to keep the family together, Rutledge advertised for a foster home in the *Star-Bulletin*, and got an immediate, heart-warming response.

I don't know how it was decided that Marie would take me to Michigan to live with her. The Prestons must have been consulted, but they were in London, halfway around the world, shocked and grieving. My grandmother, Mary Preston, was divorced and barely getting by on her own when her daughters died. My uncle John, the eldest Preston sibling, told me he remembered getting the news. "Mum and Hilary threw themselves on a bed and wept."

The second time I had an opportunity to look at Margaret's photo albums, I discovered a picture tucked in between two blank pages at the back of the last one. Dated June 1955, this picture astonished me when I first saw it: an image of my mom, Marie, in

California after the accident. It must have been the last photo Jim added to the album before boxing it up.

In this picture, Marie stands on a sidewalk in front of a house with her mother, Louise Rutledge, and her sister-in-law Alice. The house must have belonged to Marie's brother, Tom, who lived in Encino at the time. She must have gone to visit him while she was in California for the funeral. And for me.

I am being held by Louise Rutledge in this photograph. She is holding me up high, toward the camera, with her hand on my chest. She is holding me up like a trophy. In spite of the tragedy that has recently occurred, Louise looks happy, she's smiling, and apparently proud to have me in her arms.

I didn't know that Grandma Rutledge had gone on this trip with my mom until I saw this photograph. I had always imagined Marie in California alone, and somber. I imagined her having terribly conflicted feelings about the circumstances: glad to finally have a baby, but sad it has happened as the result of such a dreadful event.

It must have been the first time my mom and Grandma Rutledge flew in an airplane, a big deal in those days. Marie saved her TWA flight schedule from the trip, an artifact I found while snooping and still possess. I have held that schedule in my hands and wondered what the flight must have been like for her, the suddenness of it, the shock and anticipation.

I have also wondered what it must have been like for me, to abruptly be in the care of a stranger. Did I keep expecting Ann to appear? Did I look for her face? Listen for her voice?

In my baby book, where Ann wrote the day, date, and hour of my birth, Marie has written above it: *Friday 7-1-55 landed 7:25 pm.*

CHAPTER 7

We Are All Well and Happy Here

14 January, 1956
Brooklyn, New York

Dear Marie,

You must forgive me for not answering your letter, but as you can see by my address, I was just getting ready to leave England when it arrived. [...] I have a nice job here and the people I am with are very kind and easy to work with. I shall start saving some money and I will come and visit you in the summer. It will be lovely to see Hilary Ann. Is she starting to walk yet? I hope all goes well with you. My kind regards to your husband and best wishes for the New Year.

Very sincerely,
Mary F. Preston

My grandmother immigrated to the United States by way of an arrangement with a family from Brooklyn. They paid her way over, and she promised to work for a year as their house-keeper in return. Broke and in mourning, Mary still had three sons in their teens when she crossed the Atlantic. "I just left," she once told me. "I left the whole lot behind." Margaret and Ann had been dead for six months at this time.

22 March, 1956

Dear Marie,

[...] I am longing to see Hilary Ann and shed a few tears when I saw the snaps. Sorry the little frock was so small, but it was an inexpensive one so no loss. She must be a lovely baby to be so big. You must be taking good care of her. In the snaps you sent of her taken last September she looks very like Ann at that age.

The people I work for are quite kind, but life on the whole is quiet. I go into New York every Thursday and visit the only friends I have made here. I hope to visit my brother-in-law in Canada in July. They live in Toronto. I shall come and see you on the way there.

Best wishes to you all and a kiss for Hilary,
Mary F. Preston

P.S. Have posted the form for guardianship back to your solicitor.

It's hard for me to imagine my grandmother and my mom spending time together. Mary Preston thrived on the arts, and always surrounded herself with colorful, eye-catching objects. In contrast, my mom enjoyed watching TV and playing bingo. Beloved by her family and friends, Marie was a good cook and a generous woman, but she did not read books, go to museums, or give much thought to what her home looked like.

Mary Preston visited Wyandotte twice in 1956, and my aunt Hilary Preston visited in 1958. My mom sponsored Hilary Preston's entry into the country.

7 January, 1957
156 Montague Street
Brooklyn, New York

My dear Marie,

Please forgive me for not writing to you before to thank you for having me for Xmas and giving me such a lovely time. Everything has gone well since I got back. I have got my own apartment, very small, but just where I wanted to get one.

[...] Have you heard anything from London yet about Hilary's immigration papers? What news is there of Jimmy and the kids? And how is Lori? Bigger than ever I suppose—and how is Butchy Dog? Still the most important thing around? Don't forget to let me have the Xmas snaps when they come out. My kind regards to Syl, and your mother.

Yours affectionately,
Mary P.

I found my grandmother's letters in the window seat with all the others, and also a few from Hilary Preston. The letters from Hilary were written in pencil on unusual blue stationery that folds up into an envelope.

London
30 January, 1957

Dear Marie,

[...] I have sent in all my papers and the only thing left to do is get an affidavit from you. I am sorry they ask such a lot of questions, but I promise I will never let you down. I have never been in any trouble and have a job waiting for me in New York. Mother is anxious for me to be there by the first of April.

It makes me happy to know that little Hilary is in the hands of people who love her. I am longing for the day when I will meet you and your husband and little Hilary for the first time. I am looking forward to a brand new life in the USA.

Yours,
Hilary Preston

Among the letters, I found the affidavit of support my mom filed for Hilary Preston's visa application. On this form, Marie and Sylvester stated their earnings for 1956, which were more than double the average family income for that time. The affidavit states, "Our present dependents consist only of ourselves." So I guess I was not considered a dependent. Never legally adopted, I received monthly Social Security benefit checks as Ann Preston's survivor until I was twenty-two. The checks came addressed to Marie, who was the guardian of my estate.

My grandmother wrote the following letters on stationery from the Wellington Hotel on Seventh Avenue in Manhattan.

My dear Marie,

So glad to get your letter and know that all goes well and the papers are completed. I am working at the above hotel and like it very much as the work is easy and light. It is all sitting work so I have plenty of time to read and write letters while waiting for the telephone to ring. [...] I was very amused to hear about Lori and her skates. How did you get a pair small enough, although I suppose her feet are big for her age. [...] Hope all the Aunts and Uncles and other members of the "clan" are flourishing.

Let me hear from you,
Mary

December 5, 1957

My dear Marie,

It was so nice to finally hear from you and to know you had got a new house. I would love to come and see you all for Xmas but I have my own family here this year. My son John and his wife arrived about five weeks ago.

[...] Lori must be getting to be quite a young lady by now. I am looking forward to having a really nice studio portrait of her.

March 3, 1958

My dear Marie,

Have been hoping to hear from you—did you get my little Xmas package? I also wrote to Jimmy and have had no news. Please Marie, drop me a line and let me know any news.

We are all well and happy here. Hilary has a good job now, so she is saving up to come up to see you all on her way to Canada this summer. I do hope you are keeping well and little Lori—give her a big kiss for me.

Love,
Mary

That's the end of the correspondence. I don't know why my grandmother and my mom stopped writing to each other, but I can guess. It must have occurred to my mom that I would eventually wonder who the Prestons were if they continued to visit. And what would she tell me? I don't think my mom purposely set out to hide the truth. It was more like something she just didn't know how to deal with.

I'm sure my grandmother would have liked to have a relationship with me, or at least know how I was doing, but she must have taken the hint from Marie's lack of return letters and decided to let go. As far as I know, there wasn't any further communication with my grandmother until 1969.

CHAPTER 8

It Always Seems to Be Summer

The city of Wyandotte is just a few miles southwest of Detroit, but it's more like a small town than part of a sprawling metropolis. Originally a Native American village on the banks of the Detroit River, Wyandotte has a wide main street lined with businesses, a large park along the waterfront, and several stately old homes. It is the nicest part of the area known as Downriver, and it no longer stinks, as it did in my childhood, of pre-EPA factory smokestacks and chemical manufacturing plants.

Most of the people I knew as a child in Wyandotte were Polish, Italian, or Irish. Many families were just one or two generations removed from the "old country." It wasn't uncommon to hear someone described as being "fresh off the boat." My mom said this phrase about Maria Mucci, my best friend in grade school, who had been born in Italy. When I played with Maria at her house, her mother, who spoke little English, often served me unusual foods. The first time I saw a sliced pomegranate, it struck me as incredibly weird and somewhat disturbing, though the pickled pigs' feet I ate at home seemed perfectly normal.

As a child, I knew some Polish words but didn't know they were Polish. I thought everyone called their rear end a *dupa*. And *dziekuje* of course, meant thank you. My mom told me she was Scottish, but that had no meaning for me. I never thought of myself as "half-Scottish." Immersed in the culture of my dad's large Polish family, I was one of them.

Most of my dad's family lived within blocks of one another in Wyandotte, and they all got together for birthdays, christenings, Communions, and holidays. I loved the big weddings with polka bands. I loved kielbasa, pierogis, and stuffed cabbage. And I loved my aunts, uncles, and cousins. But they all knew the secret about me. They knew I wasn't really their kin, and looking back, I feel deceived by that.

Being an only child and the youngest cousin made me unique in my extended family. I got a lot of attention, which wasn't necessarily a good thing. I often felt picked on for not being as well-behaved as my relatives expected me to be. "Stop making that face," my aunts and older cousins frequently demanded. "What's a matter with you?"

Their reprimands came as a sharp contrast to the unconditional love I received from my mom. Being with my mom felt as comfortable as being with an old friend. In the evenings we watched TV together—shows like *Candid Camera*, *Dr. Kildare*, and *Bonanza*, to name just a few. And on weekends, I went along with her when she shopped or went visiting.

My mom most often shopped in Wyandotte, but we went to downtown Detroit every now and then, an outing that always delighted me. I have fond memories of walking among the throngs of pedestrians on Woodward Avenue and admiring the window displays of the J.L. Hudson department store—a twenty-five-story building that took up a whole city block. Hudson's had everything, including an enormous toy department and men in uniform who operated the brass-gated elevators. I loved Hudson's, and I loved Detroit.

Detroit was the fifth-largest city in the United States when I was a kid, a fact I knew and took pride in. There were tall buildings, fancy restaurants, and opulent movie theaters with huge marquees. I saw *Mary Poppins* in one of these theaters—the Adams—for my tenth birthday, the only birthday of my childhood I can recall. After the movie, we had dinner at Victor Lim's, where I had egg rolls and felt enormously sophisticated.

Detroit meant Motown, and I was proud of that, too. I had a lot of Motown hits in my record collection—a pile of 45s I wish I still owned. My mom bought me new records whenever I asked, and I spent a lot of time in our basement playing them. There I would be: an oversized girl with scabby knees, lip-syncing along and choreographing dance routines.

I enjoyed being by myself in the basement. I never felt lonely. But I just as happily played outside; that's where the scabby knees came from. I tried to play as rough as the boys on my block, getting mad if they wouldn't let me on a side when they played war, or if they climbed up trees, for which I had no skill.

Our neighborhood bordered a small industrial zone, which is why mechanical rhythms and oily scents sometimes inspire nostalgia in me. A factory across the street from our house made hubcaps in a one-story building with many square green windows, and the sound of presses, stamping out hubcaps, saturated the streets where we played. The sound was a constant, gentle *sha-shoom pom pom. Sha-shoom pom pom.* The comforting sound of *home.*

We lived four blocks from the Detroit River, so we also heard the low, soulful sound of freighters. And in summer we heard the Boblo boats—big old steamships that made excursions between Detroit and an amusement park on a downriver island. The Boblo boats made stops at the dock in Wyandotte along the way to load or unload passengers, blowing their whistles with each coming and going.

In a vivid fragment of childhood memory, my mom stands at the sink washing dishes. A stream of water runs from the faucet, and dishes clink as they're rinsed and then stacked on the counter. I am at the table, reading the comics, when I hear a long, deep *whoooo* from one of the boats and look up. I catch my mom's eye. "Boblo boat," we both say. Then she puts her hands back in the suds.

Some parts of Wyandotte haven't changed since my childhood, but the hubcap factory is gone, our house has been torn down, and the Boblo boats abandoned. I moved away from Wyandotte at the age of twenty-four, but it still feels like home whenever I go there. And this sense of home makes me wonder where I might have ended up if the accident hadn't happened. I wonder what place I'd think of as home in that case.

I'm sure many things about me would be the same no matter where I lived, but place has certainly shaped me. The blocks between the railroad tracks, Third Street, Mulberry, and Spruce are a territory I still occasionally inhabit in dreams. I know all the alleys, yards, and shortcuts. And I can still say the names of the Affholter boys in one quick breath: *Dennis-Mike-John-Jerry-Mark-Tim-Pat.*

When I think of my childhood I think of those boys, and it always seems to be summer. I remember long, lazy days with droning mowers, kids on bikes, barking dogs, and cars going by with rock and roll loud on their radios. I remember the pleasures of summer: ice-cold glasses of strong purple Kool-Aid, going high on the swings, and swimming.

We had a pool in our yard, an extravagance in our neighborhood. A round above-ground pool, it might have been only three or four feet deep and maybe six feet across, but it was plenty big for me, since I often had it all to myself. I contentedly floated and kicked around for hours, lost in my own imagined worlds.

When my parents were at work in the summer, my teenage cousin, Betty Jean, usually babysat for me. But sometimes I had to be with Aunt Katie, my dad's middle-aged, unmarried niece. Katie was technically my cousin, but I called her "aunt," as I did many of my older cousins.

"You live like pigs," Katie often said when she babysat at our house. She would haul me around and make me help her clean up. I would have to empty the overflowing ashtrays, dust the furniture, and vacuum all the bits of Kleenex on the floor. Our crazy Chihuahua chewed Kleenex. He would steal discarded wads, take them under the dining room table or behind the couch, and chew them up, leaving bits of tissue all over the rugs, which Katie found appalling. "Filthy animal!"

Aunt Katie ran a beauty shop in the basement of her house, a converted storage room paneled in knotty pine. The beauty shop had been outfitted with a hair-washing sink, two black dryers, a barber chair, and a mirror. Katie wore smocks and slacks when she worked and seemed to always have her hair set in bobby pins.

She would tie a babushka up over the pins with her long, bony fingers. She'd tie the babushka tight at the top of her head, above her unhappy, angular face.

Sometimes when Aunt Katie babysat, I had to be at the beauty shop with her while she worked, and I'd be miserable. The place reeked of permanent wave solution, and I had nothing to do but look at old hairdo magazines or listen to her talk to her customers in Polish. Katie switched to Polish when she didn't want me to know what she was saying, but I could tell when she was talking about me. The customers would glance my way and go, "*Tsk, tsk.*"

I came to hate the sound of Polish, though English wasn't much better on Katie's tongue. "Why don't you take care of your fingernails? Look at them, filthy! What's a matter with you? A big girl like you. What are you gonna do when you bleed, let it run down your legs? Achhhh! Somebody's gotta straighten you up. Tell you what's what."

She'd scrub my hair and comb out the knots, smacking my head if I didn't sit still.

"I hate her!" I complained to my mom.

"Lori! Don't say that."

"But it's true. I hate her. I hate her!"

"Just be a good girl. Okay?" My mom would make it up to me. She would buy me something special, a toy or a treat. We might stop at the dime store soda fountain for hot-fudge sundaes, and I might get to pick out some new outfits for my Barbie dolls while we were there.

Thankfully, Aunt Katie didn't babysit often. It was usually Betty Jean, who told knock-knock jokes and liked to sit in the sun rubbing baby oil on her legs. Those were the good days, with hot dogs boiled in a pan of water for lunch, and a big bag of fresh potato chips. We would eat at the picnic table in the yard. Then I'd jump back into the pool and spend the afternoon pretending to be a mermaid or a deep-sea diver.

Most of my childhood fantasies involved being famous or fabulous in one way or another: a singer, a dancer, or a dramatic actress. I occasionally took bows from the loading dock of the factory across the street, and I liked to draw proscenium stages—an inclination that must have come from my genes. I had never seen a play, except for maybe on TV, but I could not imagine a more thrilling thing.

I discovered children's magazines—*Highlights* and *Playmate*—at the doctor's office and convinced my mom to get me subscriptions. I especially liked *Playmate* because it had play scripts in it. I would hang a blanket over the clothesline in the backyard to serve as a curtain, assemble a cast, and direct rehearsals based on these scripts. I took my backyard theater seriously and became exasperated with kids who lost interest, acted silly, or wouldn't do it *my* way.

I was a girl who knew what she wanted and expected to get it, but my aunts and cousins called me *spoiled*—a horrible word I hated to hear. *Spoiled* means something is ruined. It's no good. Garbage. They called me this awful word because my mom always gave me whatever I wanted, and because there were never any consequences to my behavior. But I didn't know any other way of being, and their condemnation hurt.

My cousin Jane remembers being jealous of me when we were kids, a fact I had *no* idea of at the time. Her jealousy sprang from my abundance of clothes and toys and a fancy canopied bed from

Sears. I had a pool in my yard, a bike, and vacations—not a particularly privileged life, but a good life in Jane's eyes, and one I hardly seemed to appreciate. I took things like clothes and toys and vacations for granted. I would have been astonished at the idea of anyone being jealous of *me*.

Taller than all the kids my age, including the boys, I felt physically huge and strange. I got teased at school, got bad grades on my report cards, and had a dim awareness of something, *something*, not quite right.

I remember lying on my mom's bed with her one summer afternoon when I was only five or six. She had fallen asleep, cuddled close to me, and I wondered if our hearts were beating in unison. Since I had come from her, I thought our hearts would beat at exactly the same time. It seemed to me that *if* our hearts were beating at exactly the same time it would *prove* she was really my mom. So even then I had a primal suspicion, though it was not a thing I could name.

Search Journal March 17, 2006

I finally Googled the Las Vegas radio station, KORK, and discovered it is now a sports station. I was going to send a letter to the station asking about the photo of Jack Kogan with my mother on Fremont Street, but during my research I came across a man named Jeff Frailer—Jack Kogan's nephew!

Jeff is the host of a radio show on KLAV in Las Vegas. I sent him an e-mail about the picture of my mother with his uncle and he responded yesterday. "It's a great photo of two good-looking youngsters. Maybe the brick will identify the casino. We'll see."

I have learned that Jack Kogan hosted a television show in Las Vegas for many years. He died in 1999, which makes me sorry I didn't look him up a lot sooner. Today I got an e-mail from Jeff Frailer's sister. "Jeff forwarded the photo you sent to him. I would love to learn more. I was very close with my uncle. What was your mother's connection to Uncle Jack?"

I wrote back and told her I didn't think my mother had any relationship with Jack other than the photo. But it made me wonder.

Books about the history of Las Vegas have been absorbing my time, and I have also been listening to a CD of vintage Vegas musical recordings—finger-snapping, upbeat music that transports me in time and increases my wish to know where the KORK photo was taken. It would be so nice to be able to imagine my mother in a specific place, a place that might still be there.

March 23, 2006

I got another e-mail from Jeff Frailer this morning: "Sorry about your beautiful mother. Jack went on to have a long life. He didn't have a lot of money, but lived like a millionaire. All the maître d's in town knew him from TV. He hung out with Mr. Sinatra in the famous Sands steam room, had dinner with Rickles, Dangerfield. Name them, Jack probably interviewed them. As for the photo, the bricks and the window are the key."

It has occurred to me that Jack Kogan could be my father. But I doubt it. I'm sure my mother posed for the photo with Jack just because he was a local celebrity, and that's all there is to it. But I can't rule Jack out without knowing for sure. I want to ask Jeff and his sister what they think of the possibility, but I'm uncomfortable with the insinuation—the *accusation*.

It sure would be interesting if Jack turned out to be my father, though. What a great story that would make: my dad hanging out with Sinatra in the steam room of the Sands. I dwelled on this scenario for a little while today, even though I recognized it as a kind of "family romance fantasy."

According to what I've read about the psychology of adoption, the family romance fantasy is a common part of normal childhood development. It occurs when children doubt their biological connection to their parents, and imagine their "real" parents in some idealized way. This fantasy is usually resolved during adolescence, but can go on much longer for adoptees. When you don't know your biological family, you naturally wonder what they might be like. And it's pleasurable to imagine them in a positive way.

I have imagined my father as handsome and smart. I have imagined him as somebody special, maybe a jet pilot, but in any case, an interesting guy, a guy to be proud of. I don't blame him for anything or want anything from him, I just want to know who he is. I would like to know what family I come from. My heritage. Ethnicity. History.

March 29, 2006

Today I searched for John and Mary Valverde. I have always been curious about this couple because there is a congratulations card from them pasted into my baby book. Sometime in the late 1970s I looked them up in a San Jose area phone directory (found in the reference section of my local library) and impulsively called them. I hadn't yet met my grandmother, and I knew little about my mother at that time. I had a lot of questions, but hardly knew what to say once I had Mary Valverde on the line. I didn't ask if she knew anything about my father, and it flabbergasted me when she said, "You know, we offered to adopt you."

I thought about how different my life would have been in that case. I would have grown up in California, with a different mother and father, different friends and experiences. All but for a twist of fate—a different version of me.

When I looked for the Valverdes today in an online directory, I didn't find any listings for John, but found Mary, still in Sunnyvale. I wrote her number on a post-it and stuck it to my computer, but haven't been able to work up the nerve to call.

April 13, 2006

I was standing in our bathroom last week, talking to a contractor about a remodeling project, when Beth came home from work unexpectedly. It was ten in the morning and she was holding a cardboard box filled with her personal belongings.

Beth is no longer employed, and the shock of that hit us both like a punch to the gut. We have been staggering around for days now, stunned, and hanging onto one another for support. Even though I'm sure Beth will be able to find a new job and everything will be fine, our life as we knew it has come to a halt, and my work on the search has been suspended.

CHAPTER 9

An Everyday, Ordinary Part of My Home Life

Our house in Wyandotte had a distinctive smell, especially noticeable if you came in the back door, into the kitchen. It would hit you as soon as you stepped inside: a stale, rotting, old-house odor, combined with a substantial history of cigarette smoke and frying fish. I became aware of this odor in my teens, and it got progressively worse as the years went by, but always dissipated after you'd been inside the house for a while.

As a kid, our house comforted me like a tattered childhood blanket. As a teenager, the house embarrassed me. I began to wish I lived in a suburban development, like some of my cousins did then. I envied their rec rooms, patios, and bathrooms with showers.

For most of my childhood, I climbed in and out of our clawfoot tub for my bath. It had knobs printed with the words *hot* and *cold* and a big rubber plug that hung on a chain. My feet were burned in this tub when I was four, an event I remember vividly. My babysitter that day, a teenager known as Cookie, filled the tub but neglected to test the temperature. I don't remember the moment I stepped into the scalding water, but I do remember screaming as I ran from the bathroom to the living room. I sat on the arm of the couch, lifted my foot, and saw my skin hanging in shreds.

The next thing I remember is the emergency room. Nurses had to hold me down as I begged, over and over, for a bucket of ice water to plunge my feet into. Such a logical solution to the intense pain; I couldn't understand why they wouldn't bring it to me.

I spent the next few weeks in a hospital bed with bars, like a crib, which disturbed me at first. But I had a view of the river, and everyone who visited brought me a present. I enjoyed the attention I got in the hospital and, oddly, remember my stay there in a fond way. The ordeal probably traumatized my mom and Cookie more than me, though I still have the physical scars.

Our claw-foot tub got replaced by a modern acrylic version sometime in the late 1960s. We also got a tall metal shelving unit that went over the back of the toilet. When first installed, this shelving unit held folded face towels and some rose-scented dusting powder, but it eventually came to be littered with ointments, hairpins, pill bottles, an overflowing ashtray, and copies of the *National Enquirer* and *TV Guide*.

If I spent too much time in the bathroom, my dad would bang on the door and swear and stomp around. "What da god damn hell's goin' on?" I might be daydreaming in a tub heaped with Mr. Bubble, or practicing exaggerated expressions in the medicine-cabinet mirror. "Who da hell she think she is? God damn Queen a Sheba?!" My dad bathed on Sunday mornings. Standing in front of the bathroom sink, he would wash and shave—his ritual before putting on a suit and hat to go to Mass.

My mom had converted to Catholicism in order to marry my dad. She dressed up for church on Sunday mornings and dutifully filled our offering envelopes with money, but I never saw her pray, say the Rosary, take Communion, or give anything up for Lent. Not that this concerned me. In spite of my Catholic school education, or perhaps because of it, I never became much of a Catholic. The dogma never sunk in.

I stopped going to Mass during high school, and my mom stopped going as well, which infuriated my dad. He would call Marie a lazy, good-for-nothing, God damn drunk. He would say she'd gone crazy in the fucking head. But he didn't say these things on Sunday mornings; it would be later in the day, after he had a few.

My dad quit drinking whiskey in 1969. After that he only drank beer, which still got him drunk, but not stumbling, raving, passed-out-on-the-floor drunk like the whiskey did. He gave up whiskey as a New Year's resolution and never had another drop, inspired, I think, by an accident he had. He smashed into a telephone pole and walked away. Literally. He was found passed out on someone's lawn, miraculously unharmed, though the car was a wreck.

Sometimes, on Sundays, we'd take a drive into the country, which still existed nearby in my childhood and is now all built up into suburbs. We would stop at a roadside bar where I'd get a bottle of pop and some pretzels. Then we'd go down to Pointe Mouillee, a fishing-boat launch on Lake Erie. We'd pull into the gravel lot where my parents would sit in the car to watch the boats come and go and see if anything was biting. They might have brought a six-pack of beer along with them, brown bottles of Stroh's or Pabst. They'd sit in the car and drink, pleasantly passing the time, while I played around outside. If our crazy Chihuahua had come along for the ride, I'd take him for a walk on his leash. We'd go exploring—a too-big girl and her tiny, vicious dog.

I took a picture of my parents sitting in the car at Pointe Mouillee in April of 1963. It's a well-composed shot for an eight-year-old photographer. My dad sits behind the wheel, looking at me through the windshield. His cheek is puffed out with a wad of chewing tobacco, and he's holding a bottle of beer in his hand. On the passenger side, my mom's arm hangs out the window with a cigarette between her fingers. On her lap stands the dog, ears up, alert. My mom has an uncertain look on her face, like she's not quite sure she likes what I'm doing.

APR • 63

I remember my mom most often in the kitchen. I remember her at the stove, frying perch. I liked to watch as she dipped the silvery filets into egg, then into seasoned cracker meal. She would lay the fish gently in a pan of sizzling oil and lift them out a few minutes later, as crunchy as chips on the outside, flaky on the inside.

My dad worked a swing shift, so he ate dinner with us only when he was on days. If he was on afternoons, he would already be at work at dinnertime, and if he was on midnights he might still be asleep. Our evening meals were much more pleasant when he wasn't there. Sylvester Bocianowski had a fifth-grade education and a loud, argumentative demeanor.

My mom sometimes referred to him as "it."

"Don't wake it up," she might say when he was sleeping.

"Here it comes," she'd say when he was on his way into the house.

When he came in the back door and walked into the kitchen, my dad would spit tobacco into the sink and then loudly complain about whatever was bothering him that day: the steel mill, me, someone who'd pissed him off, or something he and my mom couldn't agree on. He would get mad about things he remembered one way and she remembered another. They had loud disagreements about who they knew when, where, and what happened. "You don't know what da god damn hell you're talking about!" he'd shout. "You don't know *shit*."

I heard a lot of swearing in our house. "God-damn-son-of-a-bitch" was an extremely familiar phrase to me. "Cram it up your ass" was common, too. And when he was really mad, my dad said, "Aw, go *fuck* yourself!"

By the time I was eight, my parents had been married twenty years, and they were never affectionate with one another. They never touched. My mom slept in her bedroom, my dad slept on the couch, and I couldn't imagine it any other way. I couldn't imagine them having romantic feelings for one another, in spite of pictures taken when they were young.

In one of these photos Marie stands in front of a cabin, most likely somewhere on Houghton Lake, the place my parents went hunting and fishing together before I arrived. In another photo she is in a rowboat, wearing sunglasses and happily holding up a big fish. There are pictures of her posed in woolen hunting clothes, and even a few of her with dead deer. In one photo she kneels in the snow, proudly holding a deer's head up by its antlers—an ideal match for my dad in that respect.

Nearly every picture of my dad shows him holding fish or dead animals. In some of these pictures his shirt is off, displaying a tan and muscled physique. You can see why a girl might have gone for him, in a physical way. Marie was nineteen when she married Syl, a man ten years her elder. And I wonder if the attraction was a Stanley Kowalski/Stella kind of thing. A thing that eventually lost its appeal.

I never understood why my mom stayed married. She could have gotten along fine on her own. She worked full time and took care of everything for our household—the banking, bills, insurance, appointments, all that sort of thing. I can only guess that she stayed because she was not the kind of person to make big changes in her life. She worked at the same factory for forty years and lived in our house until she died in it.

The only light in our house in the evenings came from the flickering glow of the television. If my dad wasn't at work, he would be asleep on the couch, and my mom would be in her chair drinking beer and smoking cigarettes. She occasionally fell asleep in her chair with a cigarette burning away in the ashtray, or about to fall from her fingers.

When I discovered her like this I would squash the cigarette out.

"Mom! Go to bed," I'd yell.

"Okay," she'd say. And then not move.

"Mom!" I'd shout louder.

"Get me a glass of baking soda water," she'd say.

Marie drank baking soda mixed with water as a remedy for indigestion. I would go into the kitchen, fill a glass with water, and then stir in two level teaspoons from the Arm & Hammer box that always sat on the counter. I would stir until the baking soda disappeared, then take the glass to her. But by the time I had done this, she might have already passed out in her bed or fallen asleep on the toilet.

Drinking was not a problem in my mom's life. She went to work every day, took care of our household, and visited friends and relatives, all while completely sober. It was only late in the evenings, or at parties sometimes, that my mom got drunk.

I remember one evening in particular when we were on our way home from a holiday gathering somewhere, traveling down Telegraph Road. My mom kept swerving in and out of our lane. I had to yell to keep her awake, warn her of red lights, and say, "Go!" when they turned green. It's lucky we made it home safe, but I don't remember being afraid. I remember being disgusted. I couldn't stand the sound of my mom's slurred voice, or the sight of her glassy eyes when she drank too much. Drinking made her pitiful and weak; it caused the competent mom I depended upon to disappear.

My mother disappeared.

Sometimes Marie wouldn't remember things that happened to her while drinking, but this never caused her concern. If she wobbled into some bushes or parked the car on the curb, she considered it funny. "Hoo boy, that must a' been some night!"

Both my parents drank, and their drinking disturbed me at times, but that's how it had always been, an everyday, ordinary part of my home life. In the evenings, when both of my parents were passed out in the living room, snoring away while some TV drama droned on, I would be free to do whatever I wanted. I might make a huge glass of chocolate milk, stirring in extra heaping spoons of Nestle Quik. Or maybe I would start an art project, something that involved scissors and glue and some paint I found in the basement.

Or I might just watch whatever came on television, sitting up close to the screen. I would be disappointed if the phone rang, or the dog started barking, and one or both of my parents woke up. I felt content in my own little world, contentedly enclosed in the cocoon of our dark house. It was morning and school and myself, my Hilary Bocianowski self, that I dreaded.

CHAPTER 10

The Amazing Force of Gravity

I never learned my multiplication tables because I had no interest in multiplication tables. Consequently, I fell hopelessly behind in arithmetic. In fifth grade I spent a lot of time on "Leprosy Island," a group of desks set apart from the others where all the dummies were made to sit. Our nun that year, Sister Angeline, must have thought we would become more studious in order to avoid Leprosy Island. But the humiliation made me *less* inclined to care about my schoolwork. Slouched at my desk, I often refused to answer when called upon. I'd cross my arms and stare at the floor while my classmates snickered and the nun's exasperation increased.

I flunked fifth grade. But then an idealistic nun named Sister Jeanne d'Arc insisted I be promoted to her sixth-grade class anyway. Sister Jeanne d'Arc said I probably just had a mental block, a term I had never heard before. I took this term as an explanation, as an *affliction*, a thing that was not my fault. Sister Jeanne d'Arc must have viewed me as a challenge, an experiment in positive reinforcement, and this briefly succeeded.

I recall standing in the kitchen, telling my mom about my promotion to sixth grade. And what I remember most about that moment is the pride I felt while telling her. I felt pride. Such a rare thing.

Unfortunately, I began sixth grade without learning what I should have learned in fifth, and then I didn't learn much in sixth because Sister Jeanne d'Arc had modern ideas about teaching. We sat in a circle, did a lot of art projects, and listened to her go off on tangents that could take up the whole afternoon.

The surplus of baby-boom students and the shortage of nuns in those days must explain why an unconventional nun like Jeanne d'Arc taught at Mt. Carmel, though she wasn't there for long. A few years later one of my classmates reported seeing her on the street in Detroit dressed as a hippie.

I entered seventh grade unable to multiply or tell a verb from a noun, a deficiency I dealt with by becoming even more withdrawn than usual. I probably did have a mental block of some kind by then. A social worker was called in to counsel me, which I regarded as another form of humiliation. "What would you wish for if you had only one wish," the social worker asked.

"To not be here talking to you," I said.

During the week of Easter vacation that year, I got to stay home by myself instead of having a babysitter or going to Aunt Katie's. And since my dad was on the day shift that week, I could watch whatever I wanted on TV. I could watch comedy shows and game shows all afternoon—the kinds of shows my dad disliked. He especially hated game shows. "God damn crazy-ass crock a' shit," he'd complain. "Nothin' but niggers and queers!"

My dad frequently demanded the TV channel be changed to one of his preferences: "Cowboys, war, or wrestling!" He would say this and then spit tobacco into the can he kept next to the couch. The couch was my dad's domain. His stinky pillows and blankets were always there, as well as his spit can, placed on some folded-up newspaper to catch the splatters and drips.

The sound of my dad spitting tobacco repulsed me, as did his vulgarity. The older I got, the more aware I became of my dad's ignorance, and the more it disturbed me. Our relationship became increasingly adversarial. When he ranted and raved, I would shout, "Shut up!" which only enraged him further. My mom begged me to just ignore him, but I couldn't. I couldn't. I cried and screamed and threw things and slammed doors. I hated my dad. And I hated the names he called me: Cow. Pig. Good-for-nothing. Piece of shit. Crazy fucking bastard.

There was no physical violence in our house. There was no sexual assault. But the obnoxious, discordant voice of Sylvester, and the constant barrage of crude words and insults, could push me over the edge. I once crushed up a pile aspirins and mixed them into Syl's beer. I didn't really think this would kill him, but I liked the idea that it might. And I liked the idea that it would be my fault. Maybe if I put aspirins into his beer and it killed him, then everyone would know how damaged I was, how crazy I had been driven by him.

I had the TV to myself that Easter week and a kitchen full of whatever I wanted to eat. My mom provided a stash of Spaghetti O's, peanut butter, Oreos, Ding Dongs, popsicles, pop, and potato chips.

"You're so lucky," my best friend Cathy said about my being an only child. There were eight kids in Cathy's family by then, with another one on the way. I envied her long blonde hair and the way she looked cute in whatever she wore. Cathy was the lucky one in my opinion.

Shapely and curvy beyond my years, and at least five inches taller than most girls my age, I had a hard time finding cool clothes in my size. I felt monstrous. Hideous. I'd started my period but didn't tell my mom. I studied the directions and diagrams inside the Tampax boxes in our bathroom, but I could not bring myself to actually try one. I used Kleenex instead, hiding my blood-stained underwear in a dresser drawer—which my mom eventually discovered.

"Why didn't you tell me about this?" She stood with her hands on her hips while I turned away in shame. The next day she bought me a big box of Kotex and a "sanitary belt." There were no peel-and-stick strips in those days. You had to wear an elastic band around your waist with metal clips attached, front and back, to keep the giant pad in place. "Here," Marie said, "use these," with no further explanation or consolation.

Cathy came over one day during that Easter week in 1967 and we practiced dancing in front of my mom's dresser mirror, a big rectangular mirror we could see our whole selves in. Cathy looked great in a white blouse and knee-length denim shorts that hugged her slim thighs. Standing next to her, I felt like a blimp. My hair had recently been cut into a bob with bangs that I regretted, and I could hardly zip my corduroys.

When we found the baby book that afternoon, time stood still. There is no other way to describe it. I can still see that moment so vividly in my memory: the baby book in my hands and the birth announcement taped onto the first page. If that moment were a photograph it would be a square color snapshot of the two of us sitting on the edge of my mom's bed, my mouth hanging open, and Cathy looking confused.

The discovery surprised Cathy, but for me it was more like confirmation of something I had always somehow *known*. The knowledge had lurked on the periphery of my consciousness like a half-remembered dream. I finally understood why I didn't look like anyone in my family. And I felt glad to know I was not my father's daughter. From that moment on, I didn't have a father.

I put the baby book back on the shelf, swore Cathy to secrecy, and then went along as if nothing had happened, though everything had changed.

I have no memories of the days and weeks following my discovery, but I do remember that summer. A race riot erupted in downtown Detroit that July, and hippies celebrated the Summer of Love in San Francisco. But for me it was all about a two-week vacation with my mom and two weeks at camp.

I went to Guardian Angel Camp, a Catholic camp run by nuns in Holly, Michigan, for three summers in a row, and I loved it. The nuns at camp were friendly and fun-loving. They were like the nuns sometimes depicted in movies and on TV, the kind who are good at pitching balls and swinging bats—butch nuns, probably lesbians, though deeply repressed.

Guardian Angel Camp had all my favorite things: swimming, skits, arts and crafts, and even a little canteen where I could buy candy and comic books. The cottages were lined up in a row, one for each age group. That summer I was in the eldest group, and I liked getting to know new girls, mostly from Detroit's northern suburbs. One of these girls brought along the Beatles' newest album—*Sgt. Pepper*—and we listened to it over and over, which is why songs from that album always remind me of camp. "Lucy in the Sky with Diamonds" brings back the wide clear lake, towering pines, and screen doors that squeaked when they opened, then shut with a smack.

I must have given *some* thought that summer to the astonishing secret I had recently discovered, but I don't remember doing so. I don't remember thinking about it or being bothered by it, but one day a nun sat next to me on a lawn swing and said, "Is something troubling you?"

I was taken aback by this. I sincerely had no idea what she was talking about. Even now, I wonder what triggered her concern. Was it my slouching? My facial expression? People often told me to stand up straight and stop frowning. But that had been going on long before I found the baby book.

My mom always took a vacation in summer, at least two weeks, and we always went somewhere, but never with my dad. He took his time off from the steel mill in the fall to go deer hunting; it didn't seem odd to me that he didn't come with us. I couldn't imagine my dad doing anything as civilized as visiting a tourist site, eating in a restaurant, or swimming in a motel pool. But with my mom I had traveled to California, New York, Washington, D.C., Niagara Falls, and several times to northern Michigan.

Some of my best childhood memories are of stretching out like a queen in the roomy backseat of a Pontiac. I would contentedly watch the scenery and billboards go by, enticed by all the tourist traps. On the way up north, billboards demanded, "See Sea Shell City!" and how could you resist? It disappointed me to discover that Sea Shell City was just a gift shop and not an actual city made out of sea shells. But there were plenty of other roadside attractions, like the Paul Bunyan Lookout, Chippewa Totem Village, and, best of all, Mystery Spot. "Experience the amazing force of gravity!"

A labyrinth of ramshackle rooms that played tricks with your equilibrium, Mystery Spot intrigued me. I knew the illusion had something to do with how it was built, but I always half-believed the "theories" about magnetized mineral deposits, fallen meteorites, and the deflection of gravitational forces.

"You don't want to go in that crazy place again," my mom would say, but I'd talk her into it. We'd pull into the lot with all the other cars full of vacationing families, some from other states. There would be moms in cotton dresses and dads in belted shorts and sport shirts. They posed for pictures in front of the gift shop, the kids squinting and poking one another.

Inside Mystery Spot, tour guides led the way and demonstrated astonishing things. Balls rolled uphill! People stood at impossible angles, and their height seemed to change. You could walk up the wall or sit on a chair balanced on its hind legs, your feet dangling in midair. My mom complained that it made her dizzy, but I thought it was great fun. Like diving into water, or twirling around on a swing, it changed your perception of things.

Cathy came along on our car trip that summer, as did Grandma Rutledge and our Chihuahua. We went all the way up to Sault Ste. Marie, and then back home by way of the Lake Michigan shoreline, where we went for an exhilarating dune buggy ride. Cathy and I ate a lot of fudge. We read comic books and teen magazines, and I took pictures with my Swinger, a groovy Polaroid camera that made rectangular black-and-white pictures which developed in a few minutes.

You had to rub a tube of fixative over these pictures after they developed, so many of my old Swinger photos have streak marks or have faded badly, but they are the only photos I have of certain people and places. That summer I took pictures of Cathy, her sister Donna, and two girls from school, Judy McDermott and Carol Kroll. I had become friends with Judy and Carol, troubled girls like me, in seventh grade, and I began hanging out with them more often than Cathy.

That fall, I entered eighth grade, turned thirteen, and learned how to smoke with Judy and Carol while walking along the railroad tracks. We had a seriously neurotic nun that year, Sister Florian, a tall, angry wasp of a woman—a woman clearly on the edge of a breakdown. Flo was prone to shrieking and swatting and slamming things around, without regard to whom or what or why.

Sometime during that school year, I told Judy and Carol about finding my baby book, the most intriguing story I had to tell about myself, and they were enthralled. They started calling me

Preston, in the way we called our classmates by their last names: McDermott, Rossetti, Belecki. I had never been called by my last name. There is no pleasurable rhythm in saying Bocianowski. I loved being called Preston. It seemed to me an especially cool name. But then a terrible thing happened.

I had been doing my homework in the kitchen one night, books and papers spread all over the table, when the phone rang and I jumped up to get it. We had a wall-mounted phone in our dining room, our only phone, with a long curly cord that hung to the floor. I picked up the receiver and pulled it into the living room, sprawling out in a chair to talk with whoever it was.

I had been talking a long time, laughing and twirling the phone cord around, when my mom called my name. "I gotta go," I said. I hung up, walked into the kitchen, and saw my mom standing there with a note from Judy McDermott in her hand—a note with the salutation *Preston*.

"How do you know this name?" she asked.

My heart thumped with fear. I couldn't move. I couldn't speak.

"Did somebody tell you this?"

I stood still and looked down at the dirty linoleum floor. This horrible moment was all my fault. *My fault!* Judy had given the note to me that day in school, and I had left it there on the table with my papers and books.

"Lori? How do you know this?"

I ran to my room, threw myself on the bed, and pulled a pillow over my head. I couldn't cope with what had just happened. I felt an overwhelming mix of embarrassment, fear, regret and shame. I wanted to erase the scene that had just occurred in the kitchen and never, *ever* have to talk about it. But my mom came into my room and sat next to me. "Lori," she said affectionately. She put her hand on my back and I pulled away.

"Leave me alone," I said. But she didn't move. She sat on my bed and told me things I desperately wanted to know, but dreaded hearing her say. I kept the pillow over my head and listened as she told about my mother being killed in a car accident with Benny and Jane's mother—the first I knew of this. Shocking news. Until that moment, I had imagined my mother being *out there*. Somewhere. Existing. With the possibility that she might one day materialize.

My mom said how sorry she felt that she never told me the truth. She said how much she loved me, told about how she had gone to California to get me. "You were such a beautiful baby," she said. "I loved you as soon as I saw you." She begged me to talk to her about it, but I wouldn't. I wouldn't look at her. I couldn't.

I didn't want to show my face, my guilty face. I had snooped. I had gotten caught. And I had caused my mom distress. Terrible, terrible. I could hardly look at her after that night because of my shame. I sulked and brooded and kept to myself—behavior my mom took personally.

"Why are you doing this to me?" she asked.

She must have thought I was angry at her, but I wasn't. I wasn't mad. I was *thirteen*. And I literally didn't know who I was. Lori Bocianowski was a lie, and Hilary Preston a mystery.

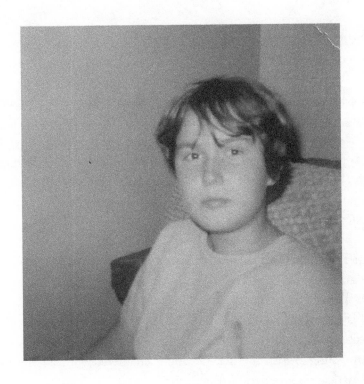

Search Journal: May 23, 2006

I sent a copy of the photograph of my mother with Jack Kogan to the Nevada State Museum and Historical Society a couple of weeks ago. I asked if they could identify the casino in the photo and got this reply from a curator: "The only real clue I have is the brickwork on the outside of the building; unfortunately, several casinos along Fremont Street had similar-looking brick, including the Boulder Club and the El Cortez, so I can't make a good judgment. If you send me your mother's name and any other possible information, it might help."

I replied to this e-mail and then received a letter a few days later informing me that the museum would like to add the photograph to their collection. They sent me a "Deed of Gift" form to fill out and send back, which I gladly did. I am happy to know this picture of my mother will live on as part of a historic collection—part of the history of Las Vegas. It's nice to think of my young British mother, no doubt enamored with all things American, now a part of Americana.

Yesterday I got a notice in the mail that a certified letter from Fallon Naval Air Station was being held for me at the post office. I felt certain the letter would simply be an acknowledgement of the Freedom of Information Act request I recently submitted, but I couldn't help imagining a large envelope with a photocopied roster of 1954 officers inside it. I took pleasure in the daydream of how great it would be to have a list of names to investigate.

I hopped in the car and drove to the post office in the middle of a rainstorm, feeling optimistic. A buoyant piece of classical music played on the radio, and I turned it up. But the letter I signed for when I got to the post office came in an ordinary business envelope and didn't seem to contain much.

I ran back to my car without an umbrella, the letter clutched to my chest, and opened the envelope as soon as I got inside. I scanned the official government language to the middle of the third paragraph. "We were unable to locate responsive documents to your request. The retention requirements for the records being sought are for two years."

I tossed the letter onto the passenger seat, started the car, and turned the radio off. I felt tremendously disappointed, even though I hadn't really expected my request to be filled so easily. I drove down the street with only the sound of my windshield wipers flapping and felt a sudden stab of heartache for my unknown father. I *felt* the loss of him—something I had never experienced before – and I feared his potential permanent loss if I am unsuccessful at this search.

I came home and tried to explain my sudden feeling of paternal loss to Beth, but she was absorbed in an online job application. The unemployment situation is not as grim as it first seemed. We are adjusting, though it is not an easy or happy adjustment. Beth is understandably distracted, and we are experiencing a bit more togetherness than either of us desires.

CHAPTER 11

Other Family

In the summer of 1969, I saw the launch of Apollo 11, the first manned mission to the moon. I saw it from the hood of my cousin's car in Cocoa Beach, Florida—or as close to Cocoa Beach as we could get. We were somewhere on the side of the road with thousands of other cars, and it's the image of the traffic jam more than the rocket launch that sticks in my memory. Cars were parked alongside the road for miles and miles, with license plates from all over the country. Some people had set up folding chairs and picnic coolers, and there were a lot of people with cameras and binoculars, all aimed toward Cape Kennedy, a place so far in the distance I could only imagine it.

My mom had taken me and Cathy on a road trip to Florida for our summer vacation that year, stopping to see the Smoky Mountains along the way. We went to visit my cousin Linda, and her husband, Ed. Their house in Miami had shag carpeting, hanging lamps, colorful throw pillows, and sliding glass doors. Linda and Ed were more stylish than anyone else in my dad's family and I adored them. Ed worked for Eastern Airlines, which is how they ended up in a place as far away and glamorous as Miami.

On the day of the launch, we got up before dawn to arrive there on time. The rocket went up at 9:30 a.m., but there really wasn't much to see as we turned our faces into the bright morning sun, shading our eyes with our hands. We heard the countdown on the radio, heard the roar, but the rocket was so far away we could hardly see it. We watched as the contrail disappeared. Then we drove back to Ed and Linda's.

Although the launch was somewhat anticlimactic, it must have made an impression on me. When we got home, I wrote to my grandmother, Mary Preston, about our vacation to Florida and the launch of the rocket. I had gotten her address from Benny. He was in Vietnam, and we were corresponding. He sent me her address in one of his letters and suggested I write to her. The address he gave me was for a place in Ossining, New York, called the Victoria Home.

Two years had gone by since I discovered the baby book, and my curiosity about my biological relatives had grown. But I never talked about it. Complicit in the illusion of my identity, I didn't ask questions because it would have meant acknowledging my other self. The trick revealed. The artifice exposed.

On the rare occasions when my mom mentioned the Prestons or referred to me as her *adopted* daughter, I would be appalled. How could she just casually pull back the curtain like that? It made me uncomfortable, but I could not have told you why.

Now I know it is common for adoptees to feel a strong sense of loyalty to their adoptive parents, a loyalty that can feel like a heavy responsibility. Many adoptees instinctively feign disinterest in their biological family so as not to disappoint their adoptive parents or threaten their place in their adoptive family.

I have no memory of writing to my grandmother but clearly recall the moment I got a letter from her in return. I was sprawled on the floor in front of the TV on a Saturday afternoon, watching *American Bandstand*, when the letter landed in front of me. My mom, who had just come in from getting the mail, tossed it there. "Something for you," she said and continued on her way into the dining room.

The letter had no return address, but the postmark, Ossining, made my heart skip a beat. I knew this letter had come from my grandmother. *My grandmother.* I could hardly believe I was holding a letter from her in my hand. I took it to my room, shut the door, and ripped it open.

August 10, 1969

My dear Lori,

Thank you for your letter and nice snapshot—you sound as if you had a wonderful holiday and most exciting to see the rocket go up.

Well, Lori, I hope you realize what a very lucky girl you are to have been chosen for safekeeping and to be loved by Marie and Syl. Also all your other relations in Michigan. As you get older you may meet some of your other family but your first loyalties must be to the Michigan clan.

Nice to know you are writing to Benny. I owe him a letter so must get down to it. Tell your Uncle Jim that I have had a letter from Billy, he is in the British Navy and is going on a lovely cruise for a year and will be putting in Pearl Harbor and San Francisco.

What part of Florida were you in? Do you go every year? Your Uncle Timothy has been visiting his relatives in Canada and I have given him your address so perhaps he will take a spin down and see you. […] My very best wishes to your Mum and Dad and all the clan—keep well and happy.

With affection,
Your Grandma "P"

I felt thrilled to get a letter from a person actually related to me. I could hardly believe she was really *my* grandmother. She used so many odd words and phrases: "a wonderful holiday," "your first loyalties," "the Michigan clan," "the British Navy," "a lovely cruise," "a spin down," "your Mum and Dad." Nobody I knew said things like that. It fascinated me. And there was that tantalizing prospect: "As you get older you may meet some of your other family."

Other family.

I had a whole other family, a family who said things like *a wonderful holiday*. And they were not just an abstract other, but real people doing real things. They were living their lives at the very same moment I sat in my room with this letter in my hands trying to imagine them.

I felt awed by this concept, but I didn't much care for the part of the letter about how lucky I was to have been "chosen" by Marie and Syl. I didn't feel lucky at all. I had been kicked out of Mt. Carmel at the end of eighth grade and then barely survived a horrendous year at a public junior high school.

My grandmother included a photograph with her letter, a picture in which she is standing at the far end of a wide stretch of lawn, with the Hudson River and hills in the distance. I couldn't make out any details of her face, and I didn't know why she lived at a place called the Victoria Home. *Was it an old-age home?*

My mom never asked about the letter. I had two pen pals then, one in California and the other in England. I had signed up for them in teen magazines. So it wasn't unusual for me to get a letter. When I finished reading, I stashed it within the pile of books and magazines I kept next to the armchair in my cluttered bedroom.

That armchair, a big green relic that had been in our living room during my childhood, is where I spent a lot of my time as a teenager, listening to the radio, reading, writing in my diary, and daydreaming. I sat in that chair and read the letter from my grandmother again and again, but I never wrote back and I'm not sure why. Perhaps I felt a little intimidated by her, or I just didn't know what else to say. In any case, the letter eventually got lost among my things. I started high school. The sixties became the seventies. And I soon became distracted by romance and rock and roll.

I played albums by The Doors, Cream, and Jimi Hendrix over and over on my stereo. "Jigaboo music," my dad complained. "God damned *Gypsy* music!" My dad used the word Gypsy in a derogatory way, and often as a way to describe me, especially if I wore colorful clothes. "Gypsy!" He spat the word.

My mom let me go to Cobo Hall in Detroit to see Jimi Hendrix when I was fifteen. I begged for tickets and so she got them, not just for me, but Cathy too. She drove us to Cobo the night of the concert, dropped us off at the curb, and there we were: a couple of naive Downriver girls wearing our first pairs of bell-bottom blue jeans. We walked into the swirling psychedelic scene.

I knew who I was in high school. I was a "freak," and proud of it. My high school years were not too bad. I did okay academically and finally got to be in some plays—a thrilling experience for me. As corny and cliché as it sounds, I felt like my true self for the first time in high school theater. I felt like I belonged, a unique feeling for me.

Debbie Murphy, who had the lead in every play we did, received a scholarship to study theater in college, and this made me deeply envious. My guidance counselors had steered me toward the most basic classes, classes for students not expected to go on to higher education.

I didn't know anyone who went to college, and I had never considered it as a possibility for myself. But I enrolled at Henry

Ford Community College, partly because I could continue to receive Social Security survivor benefits if I stayed in school, and partly because I didn't know what else to do with myself.

HFCC had a little theater department, in which I quickly became involved. I fell in with a group of creative friends, moved into an apartment, and enjoyed a few years of relatively carefree independence, without a clue or any plans for the future.

CHAPTER 12

California

Every important thing in my life came to an end or went wrong in the spring of 1976. After attending community college for three years, I had not managed to earn a degree or develop any marketable skills. I appeared in my last play at HFCC, broke up with my boyfriend, had an abortion, and parted ways with my roommate, my best friend, on bad terms. My creative gang went their separate ways and I moved back into my parents' house, where I slept and cried a lot.

I sat sobbing at my mom's kitchen table one day that June as she sat across from me, glaring at me with disdain. Her hands shook as she lit a cigarette, inhaled deeply, and then blew the smoke out her nose. "You're such an *actress*," she said, and this hit me like a slap in the face. Marie had become a stranger who didn't understand me and took my unhappiness personally. She wanted to know why I was making *her* life so miserable.

"I just want to get out of here," I said. "I want to go away on a train."

I had a pamphlet about a special ticket offered by Amtrak—a USA Rail Pass—which allowed unlimited access to their passenger trains for two weeks. You could go wherever you wanted without a plan, and this sounded ideal to me. I loved the idea of traveling without an itinerary, and love it still, though I have rarely had the opportunity to do so.

Cathy had gotten married and lived south of Los Angeles, so I told my mom I wanted to go to California and visit her. "Good idea," she said. "Maybe you can find some kinda' job out there." My mom bought the USA Rail Pass and gave me some traveling money as well, no doubt glad to be rid of me and my weeping.

I called Cathy to tell her my plan, then loaded up the large frameless backpack I used for camping trips. Along with essentials, I tucked in some of the old letters and photographs I'd found in the window seat. Curiosity about my biological identity had lain dormant during my prolonged adolescence, but now I wanted to know more. I wanted to go to California and investigate, though I didn't tell my mom this. She drove me to the Michigan Central train depot in Detroit and gave me some extra spending money as we parted. Standing in the vast, decrepit waiting room of the station, she handed me the cash with a hard, unhappy look on her face. "Here," she said, "put this somewhere safe."

I stashed the money in a pocket inside my pack, and when I looked back at my mom there were tears in her eyes, something I rarely saw. Marie did not generally have highs and lows of emotion; I hadn't seen her cry since our Chihuahua died.

I leaned over to hug my mom, an awkward maneuver since I towered over her by nearly a foot, and we didn't hug often. But I hugged my mom and breathed in her scent: solder, cigarettes, and hairspray.

"Be careful," she said and walked away.

Amtrak was only a few years old in 1976, and traveling by rail was relatively new to me. I had taken the train to visit friends in Kalamazoo a couple of times and enjoyed the trip across the state. I found pleasure in the experience of solitude among strangers, alone with my thoughts as the train clattered onward. Train travel made me feel world wise. I also liked the possibility of being perceived by my fellow travelers as a successful person. They might guess me to be a college student from Ann Arbor, a young wife, or a career girl, and not just a lost twenty-one-year-old with no idea how to be an adult.

The three-day journey to California on the Southwest Limited was even better than I expected. The views were magnificent, I met interesting people, and wrote therapeutic entries in my journal. I had two seats to myself the whole way, sleeping comfortably at night by using my pack as a pillow. I washed my hair in the bathroom sink, lived on grilled cheese sandwiches, and felt progressively lighter of heart as we got farther and farther from Michigan.

I grew increasingly excited about California. *California!* My troubles fell away as I anticipated the thrill of setting foot in that legendary land so often depicted on TV and in the movies. I hadn't been out west since the trip to Disneyland in 1962, a trip I could hardly recall. I imagined California in a dreamy, idealized way—a faraway realm filled with sunshine and ocean waves. California was the setting for the story of my other self. My other, unknown, authentic self.

The train arrived in LA at dawn. I spent the day hanging out at the beautiful Art Deco Union Station waiting for Cathy's husband, Richard, to pick me up when he got off work. Wandering around the gardens surrounding the station, I fell in love with the soft California air and the many varieties of tropical plants. I ate in the diner, took some pictures, and felt content to just sit and watch people go by. When a film crew set up to shoot some scenes in the station that afternoon, I observed them with an awestruck reverence.

Cathy and Richard had dropped out of high school in the eleventh grade to get married. They found Jesus, moved to California, and had a baby. Richard did some kind of menial work, and Cathy took up sewing and quilting.

"Praise the Lord!" she said when I walked into their tiny apartment in Costa Mesa that evening. Cathy's straight blonde hair came to her knees, and she wore a cotton dress she had made herself. I hadn't seen my friend in a long time and looked forward to our visit, but she quoted scripture frequently and made an effort to convert me. I spent two uncomfortable nights on her couch, and then went on my way. I hugged her goodbye in her kitchen, and that was the last time I saw her, though we exchanged letters for several years before losing touch.

I boarded the Coast Starlight and headed north, enjoying glorious views of the Pacific along the way, past Santa Barbara and San Luis Obispo, toward San Jose, the city of my birth. Ever since finding my baby book, I had been intrigued by the idea of San Jose—such an unusual birthplace for a Downriver girl. It had become mythic in my mind, more imaginary than actual. So when the train pulled into the station late that afternoon and I saw a sign that said, "Welcome to San Jose," I felt overwhelmed by the concrete fact of it.

My mother lived here. My mother lived here with me.

Long-suppressed emotions came to the surface as I stepped off the train. Tears ran down my cheeks as I looked around, trying to grasp the fact that I was actually there. Lugging my backpack, I was most likely wearing a thin cotton bohemian top of some sort and cut-off jean shorts, which attracted the attention of a sweet-talking creep. A long-haired guy wearing a suit jacket with jeans offered to take me anywhere I wanted to go. I had a hard time brushing him off, and as I walked away he called me a bitch.

Welcome to San Jose.

I decided to stay in a motel for a few days and checked into the San Jose Lodge, an L-shaped place with two stories of rooms that faced a parking lot and a small pool. I don't remember how I ended up at this motel, but I still have a souvenir postcard of it. The double bed felt luxurious compared to train seats and Cathy's couch. I stretched out and fell into a sleep so deep I woke up disoriented, unable to discern the time of day or my location. When I finally remembered: *San Jose*, it delighted me.

I found a place to eat, picked up a bus schedule, and set off to explore. I had torn a map out of the phonebook in my room and used it to find my way to O'Connor Hospital, the place of my birth. I went directly to the hospital records office, where there was just one girl, not much older than me, at work. She stopped typing and smiled when I walked in; she seemed glad for the distraction. But when I asked for the records from my birth, the girl's expression changed. "I'm sorry," she said. She couldn't allow me to look at another person's record, even my own mother's.

Undeterred, I pleaded my case, explaining how my mother had died when I was a baby, and how I had come all the way from

Michigan just for this. I tried to sound as desperate as possible. And it worked. The office girl sighed and said, "All right." She asked for the month and year of my birth and then said, "Wait here." She went through a door at the back of the office as I paced around, full of nervous anticipation. I had no expectations about what I might discover on the hospital record, I just wanted to see it, to see into the past.

It wasn't long before the girl returned with a small dusty box in her hand which contained a reel of microfilm. She loaded the reel onto a huge contraption, a microfilm reader, which enlarged the film and displayed its contents on a screen. There were knobs that spun the film quickly backward and forward as you searched for the record you wanted. The girl showed me how to use the machine and then said, "If anyone comes in here, you've got to stop what you're doing."

I thanked her and worked as quickly as I could, easily finding my mother's hospital admission record. On this record were a few bits of information that were new to me, such as my mother's birth date and her birthplace—Gorleston, England. I took notes on a piece of scratch paper with a little stub of a pencil.

I had come to San Jose without knowing what I was looking for. I was just *looking*. And there on my birth record, on a line labeled "Name of father," something had been written, then scratched out. I stared intently at the microfilm screen. I thought the first name might start with an *S*, which later helped fuel my Stanley conviction, and one of the letters in the last name had a tail that hung below the writing line—a *Y* or *G* or *J*. This tantalizing name was right in front of my eyes, yet I couldn't decipher it.

I wondered why "Name of father" had been scratched out. Was it because my mother didn't want it on the record? Or because she wasn't married? Maybe they weren't allowed to put a father's name on the record if the mother wasn't married. But I didn't ask about that. I just stared at the scratched-out name as long as I could, thanked the girl at the counter, and went on my way. Which I regretted for many years after.

I could have stolen that microfilm, or bribed the girl for it. I could have found someone, some expert, to decipher the writing below the scratch marks. But I just walked away and left it there. And when I called O'Connor Hospital while searching for my father in the 1990s, I learned those old microfilm records had been destroyed.

I used my phonebook map to find my way to Sunnyvale. I rode a bus up El Camino Real and then began to hike up a steep hill, into the neighborhood where Jim, Margaret, and my mother had lived. I trudged along with my pack on my back, enchanted by the view of the mountains in the distance. But the walk took much longer than I expected, and it was blazing hot. When a pickup truck pulled over, I gratefully accepted a ride.

"Where you headed?"

There were two men in the truck, tradesmen of some sort.

"Six-eighty Borregas," I told them.

"Hop in," the driver said, indicating the back of the truck with his thumb.

Hitching a ride with strangers didn't seem unusual to me in 1976. Only now, looking back, does it strike me as risky behavior. I climbed onto the back bumper of the truck and hoisted myself over the tailgate. I sat down on a big metal toolbox, and it wasn't long before we pulled up across the street from the house I had looked at so often in photographs. The sudden sight of it astonished me. I got out of the truck and stood there, transfixed.

"You all right?" the guy asked.

"Yeah. Thanks." I waved at him and slowly crossed the street. Six-eighty Borregas had changed since 1954, but not much. There were bushes and trees now, and a sign hanging over the carport proclaimed, "The Hernandez Family."

I walked across the driveway where my mother and Margaret had once stood to have their photograph taken. Then I went through the carport and toward the side door, feeling as if I had entered a dream. I was in a place well-known to me, but not a place I remembered being.

I hadn't planned on going inside the house, but that's what I did that day. I knocked on the door, and a kid of about twelve or thirteen answered. The poor kid. I can only imagine how strange I must have seemed to him. An emotional stranger. I told him I had lived in this house a long time ago, when I was a baby, and I just wanted to come inside and see it.

"My parents aren't home now," he said.

"But I've come all the way from Michigan." I used the line that had worked so well in the hospital.

"Maybe you can come back later?" He cautiously held onto the door.

I told him I was only there for that day, that moment. "I've traveled all this way just to see this house." I pulled pictures out of my pack, showed him my mother holding me near the spot where we stood, the photo in which her cheek is close to mine.

He gazed at the picture and then up at me, as if he were checking my ID.

"Okay." The kid reluctantly agreed. He stepped aside and let me in.

I know I walked around inside that house but it's a blur in my memory. I know I saw the kitchen and the living room, but I felt overwhelmed, and also uncomfortable for frightening the kid. I didn't stay long. I said thanks, took a last look, walked out the door, and heard the lock click behind me.

I walked down the driveway and stood across the street. I stared at the house, the suburban block, the view of the mountains and thought: *This is what my mother saw.* I stood there with a new sense of my mother as a person—a real person I had lost.

In order to grieve her I had to fully imagine her, and I had finally begun to do that.

I spent the rest of that journey on trains. I rode up the coast, into the woodlands of Oregon and Washington, writing and thinking and talking with people along the way. In Seattle I changed direction and headed back east, back home, feeling more solid than at the trip's beginning. I had become a little more *known* to myself. Though I still had a long way to go.

Search Journal: June 23, 2006

Beth used to come home sometime around six or seven in the evening. Wearing a dark suit and sensible flats, she would walk in the door to our kitchen lugging the briefcase she calls "the black hole." Exhausted, she would want nothing more than to change clothes, pour a glass of scotch, sit down, and read the newspaper. Then she'd see me and her face would change, the tensions of her day would ease and she would exhale. "Hi honey," she'd say.

I managed a non-profit theater in Kalamazoo when we met, the most ideal job I ever had. I thought I'd easily find another position in the arts when we moved to Grand Rapids, but that didn't happen, and I settled into the role of housewife. Which I don't mind. It's an irony of our relationship that Beth is a human resources professional and I haven't been able to find work, but up until recently that's been okay.

The worst part of Beth's unemployment is that she's home *all the time.* Sharing our home-office space and our one computer is a challenge. It's understood that Beth's job search takes priority over my father search, but I still manage to get a little bit done here and there.

It surprised me when the phone rang yesterday and *Sunnyvale Medical Clinic* appeared on our caller ID. This is the doctor's office where my mother went for obstetrical care. I sent them a letter a few weeks ago asking for information, so I answered eagerly, thinking the call might be good news. But they just wanted to inform me that they don't keep records that old, and even if they did, they wouldn't release them unless I had power of attorney. I asked the woman on the phone if she could just tell me *if* they had any record of my mother, and she refused. Which really annoyed me. I hung up in a huff.

I still have several items on my to-do list that I have not yet begun to investigate, including "the woman in *People* magazine." Her picture appeared in the October 25, 1993 issue of *People*, but she isn't anyone famous. She was one of several average people profiled in an article about haircuts, which included before and after photos.

I was flipping through this issue of *People* in 1993 when I came across the haircut article. I glanced at it briefly, turned the page, and then turned it back. It took me a few moments to realize why this woman looked so familiar. I'm not accustomed to seeing people who resemble me, and looking at her was like looking in a mirror.

My look-alike's name and age were listed in a little blurb below her picture. Danielle Grise, ten years younger than me, had my dimples, my brown eyes, my wide cheeks, and my hair. I couldn't help but wonder if we were related, so I attempted to contact her.

I had my picture taken in the same pose as Danielle's "after" photo and sent it to her, along with a letter, via *People*. I asked the magazine to forward my letter to Danielle, but never got a response. Either she didn't receive my message, or she did and thought I was crazy.

July 15, 2006
I promised myself to get something accomplished on the search this month, in spite of the many distractions that have been

keeping me from it. And so I finally Googled Danielle Grise and found a recent picture of her. The similarity in our appearance is no longer immediately apparent, but I can still see a resemblance. We could easily be in the same family.

Danielle is a high school English teacher in Rhode Island. I found her picture and a profile posted on the school's website. I found her so easily it made me wonder why it takes so long for me to do these things. I am not a procrastinator by nature. And I'm not afraid of what I'll find. If anything, I'm afraid of what I *won't* find. I'm afraid of being a fool, of wasting my time on this foolish, impossible thing. When people ask what I'm doing these days, I am hesitant to say. I sometimes feel like a fairy tale child, an orphan in a thick dark forest, with only a trail of crumbs to lead the way.

I want to get in touch with Danielle but worry about coming across as some kind of stalker or weirdo. Resemblances between unrelated people happen all the time. It's a little strange that I've hung on to this issue of *People* for more than ten years. And now here I am hoping it might be the one big clue to my identity.

I really should just contact Danielle and get it over with, but I'm afraid of scaring her off. Even if she is my cousin or sister, I'm afraid she won't want to admit it. And then that will be that, a meager trail of crumbs going nowhere.

CHAPTER 13

Anonymous

I met Mike Reilly in the summer of 1974. He lived in a house full of long-haired college students in Kalamazoo that summer, though he wasn't a student himself. He worked at a psychiatric hospital, rode a motorcycle, and tended to nod off in the middle of group gatherings, which earned him the nickname "Sleepy."

I had recently broken up with one of Mike's roommates—an intense, romantic guy who drank too much. This ex-boyfriend made Mike's low-key personality attractive in contrast. At six-foot-two, with a full beard and dark glasses, Mike struck me as deep and mysterious. One evening that summer, when we were all sitting around smoking pot, I heard Mike use the word "facetious" in a conversation. I had never heard this word, had no idea what it meant, and assumed Mike to be much smarter than me. He was twenty-five, I was nineteen, and tremendously unsure of myself.

It turned out that Mike, the eldest of five brothers from a working-class family, wore dark glasses to hide a damaged eye. It had been accidentally poked with a stick by a neighborhood kid when Mike was seven. The first time I saw him without his dark glasses, the vulnerability of his sightless eye inspired a tender empathy in me.

A fan hummed in the window of Mike's room one hot afternoon as we lay on his bed—a waterbed mattress on the floor. We were having a long, intimate talk when I told him my story. I told him about finding the baby book, and this intrigued him. He told me about a similar experience that had happened to him, one he'd never shared with another soul. He cleared his throat and spoke slowly as he told me about a trip his family took when he was ten.

"We went to Missouri to see my dad's brother. We'd never met this guy and his family before, never laid eyes on them, before or after. And while we were there, one of my cousins told me I was adopted. We were playing outside and he just said it, you know: '*You're adopted.*'"

Mike later asked his mother if this was true, and she told him it was not. But he couldn't stop thinking about it. "I never felt like I belonged in my family," he said. He grew up feeling alien and odd, but never asked anyone another question about it.

"Your cousin must have been teasing you," I said.

It just didn't make sense to me. I couldn't believe that Mike's mother would have lied to him like that. And I couldn't believe he wasn't related to his brothers. I dismissed Mike's suspicion, and he rarely mentioned it again.

We were married in 1979, divorced in 1986, and have been on friendly terms since then. When our twin sons began asking questions about their ancestors, I encouraged Mike to research his family tree. I had heard a Reilly family story about being related to Buffalo Bill Cody, but Mike didn't know the details. Both his parents had passed away by then, and his extended family wasn't close.

It took a few years of prodding, but Mike finally did some investigating, which led to the discovery that he had, indeed,

been adopted as an infant. And even though he had always sus-
pected this, the fact of it distressed him deeply. He felt betrayed
because no one ever told him the truth.

"It's like my whole life has been a sham," he said, "a lie."

Mike and I had several long conversations after his discovery.
He couldn't get over the fact that his brothers were *not* his brothers. Mike learned that his mother suffered several miscarriages
before his adoption and then subsequently gave birth to four sons,
none of whom knew he was adopted.

"They've always been your brothers, and they'll always *be*
your brothers," I said. But my words didn't seem to help much.
The bedrock of Mike's identity had crumbled.

Mike's adoption had been arranged through a Catholic social service agency in Kalamazoo. After finding out about his adoption,
Mike went to this agency and was given his "non-identifying social
history." This document, written by a social worker, explained the
circumstances that led to Mike's adoption and listed the physical
descriptions, nationalities, occupations, and interests of his parents and grandparents without revealing their names.

His birth mother, twenty years old at the time of his birth,
had graduated from high school, attended college, and wanted
to be a teacher. The eldest child of seven, she kept the pregnancy
hidden from her family until she went into labor. Mike's birth
father was a twenty-one-year-old high school dropout who had
served in the army. Unemployed, he had been jailed twice for
drunkenness. Mike's birth parents knew each other for three
years and had talked about getting married, but his birth father's
religious views were "strongly anti-Catholic," and he did not wish

to convert in order to marry. He offered to help out financially, but was reported to be dating another woman shortly after Mike's birth. When Mike was one month old, his birth parents appeared before a probate judge and relinquished their parental rights.

This social history provided Mike with the kind of information I would have been grateful to know about my paternal roots, but reading it only increased Mike's distress. He became despondent, saying it upset him to learn his father had not been an admirable guy.

I knew the discovery of Mike's adoption would be hard news for our sons, too. Justin and Jeremy were tall, athletic teenagers who related easily to Mike's big, boisterous brothers. I'm sure they derived a large part of their identity from their uncles. They were *Reillys*, and it broke my heart to think about taking that away from them. I told Mike I didn't want to tell the boys about his adoption right away, and he agreed—which is how Mike and I, both persons who were not told the truth, decided to not tell the truth.

From then on, whenever one of my sons asked a question about the Reilly family history, it made me a little sad. Both Reilly grandparents had passed away, but the boys wanted to see pictures of them. They wanted to know where their grandparents had lived and what kind of work they had done. On a school trip to Gettysburg, they found the grave of a soldier named Reilly in a Civil War cemetery and posed for a picture next to his gravestone.

It fascinated me to watch my sons put this family identity together. I saw how the story of who they came from helped form the story of who they are. They had heard the Buffalo Bill Cody story and wanted to know more about it. Like most people, Justin and Jeremy accepted their genealogy as a matter of casual fact, unaware of its value in the development of their self-concept.

The presence of others with whom you share DNA and familial resemblance is no big deal if you grow up with your biological relatives. But to those without kin, this is an incredible phenomenon. When my sons were born, I looked at their familiar faces with wonder. I could hardly grasp the concept that they were really and truly biologically a part of me, my actual "flesh and blood."

It baffles me that some people don't understand the need for adoptees to know their biological relatives, or recognize the loss that comes from not knowing. Adoption experts call this loss "genealogical bewilderment." It's the sense of being cut off from your heritage. Not knowing the traits, talents, abilities, perspectives, beliefs, and history of your relatives. When people look at photographs of their ancestors, or hear their stories about them, and see parallels in their lives, it gives meaning and value to those parallels. It explains *why* they are who they are. It connects them, makes them a part of something larger—whereas those without this knowledge are alone. Anonymous.

I didn't tell our sons about Mike's adoption until they were twenty years old. It came up when they were asking questions about their grandfather again. Justin wanted to know about Jack Reilly's experience as a World War II pilot, and I knew it was time to come clean. I regretted not telling them the truth in the first place and couldn't let the deception go on any longer.

"Boys, I have something important to tell you."

These were difficult words to say, but I said them. I sat down with my sons and told them the story of their father's adoption.

As much as I hated to do it, I told the story and took away an important part of who they knew themselves to be.

This occurred during a time of transition in our lives. I had recently moved into a new house after divorcing my second husband, and my sons had temporarily flown back into the nest. They were sitting on an old couch in my basement with video game equipment and empty pizza boxes at their feet as I told them the story. And I remember the way they listened: quiet, attentive, absorbing this new information. I'm sure they were shocked, but they didn't ask many questions. They just kept saying "Huh" in an amazed, slightly angry way.

I spoke ambiguously about when their father found out, making it sound recent. I didn't tell them we'd known for six years. I was glad, at least, to be able to tell them their father's ethnicity, thanks to the social history he'd been given. But ethnicity seemed beside the point at that moment. An important part of my sons' identity had just been replaced by an unknown, a void—a disconcerting experience I knew firsthand, and felt sorry to share.

CHAPTER 14

All Good Wishes and Love

I knew Mike Reilly for five years before our wedding—five difficult years during which I struggled and failed to become the competent person I might have been. I longed for things I was ill-equipped for, and hungered for something I couldn't define; something I wasn't finding at the disco where I worked as a waitress.

Mike and I broke up and got back together several times during those years, like a bad habit we couldn't shake. We caused each other a lot of emotional harm. And *then* we got married. We had a wedding in Wyandotte, went on a honeymoon trip to Florida, and moved into an apartment in Kalamazoo, Mike's hometown.

Halfway between Detroit and Chicago, Kalamazoo is a college town, a place with an expressway and a river running through it. "It's on the *west* side of the state," I said smugly to relatives who rarely ventured far from Downriver. At the age of twenty-four, I felt glad to finally be moving on, and ready for whatever might come next.

As I packed for the move to Kalamazoo, I found the letter from my grandmother I had misplaced in 1969. Holding it in my hand again seemed like a small miracle. The picture of my grandmother standing on a lawn outside the Victoria Home remained tucked inside the envelope, and I wondered if she still lived there, in Ossining, New York.

I packed the letter into a cardboard box along with my baby book and the letters I had found in the window seat. When we settled into our apartment in Kalamazoo, I put this cardboard box into a hope chest I inherited from my mom. I kept all my personal memorabilia in this chest, and the scent of cedar that escaped when I opened it always evoked secrets and mystery.

I was seven months pregnant and still adjusting to the idea of having a baby I hadn't planned when my obstetrician preformed an ultrasound, a relatively new procedure not used routinely in those days. Lying on an examination table in a darkened room, I felt nervous and uncomfortable.

"I'll show you what I'm seeing in just a minute," the doctor said. Causing me to imagine horrifying complications as that long, long minute ticked by.

Finally, he swiveled the monitor around to show me the indistinct image on the screen. "Here's the baby's head," he said. Then he slowly moved the transducer lower on my belly. "And here's another baby's head."

What? My brain had a hard time processing this information. "You're having twins," he explained, as if this were as ordinary as having a cup of coffee.

My sons were born in January of 1981, and as soon as I saw them I loved them profoundly. Buoyed by the excitement and attention of having twins, it took a while for the exhaustion to hit me, but when it did it hit me hard. Those first three months with the boys were brutal. And we didn't have any help. Mike's mother had recently passed away, his younger brothers were bachelors, and my only close friend in Kalamazoo had a newborn infant of her own. My mom was the only person we had to rely on, and she still worked full time then.

I vividly remember sitting on the couch in our apartment the first time my mom arrived for a visit after my return from the hospital. I was trying to feed both babies simultaneously when she walked in the door, and I felt such relief. Here was my mom, my dependable mom, wearing her work clothes and a red plaid jacket. She had come directly from the factory on a Friday afternoon because she couldn't wait to hold my baby boys in her arms.

Marie stayed for a week, and came to visit often for weekends after that. But I spent most of my time alone with the babies while Mike worked, went out with his friends, or fell asleep with the TV on. Feeling lonely and lost, I joined a support group for new mothers at the YWCA. One of the volunteer leaders of this group, a woman named Mary Powell, provided the emotional support I desperately needed. The wife of a doctor, with two small children of her own, Mary found the time to visit me, help with the boys, listen, and offer wise advice for which I am still extremely grateful.

I talked to Mary about my grandmother, and she encouraged me to make contact.

"I'm sure she'd be glad to hear from you."

"I don't know..." I said.

"What are you afraid of?"

I couldn't say. The idea of communicating with my grand-mother had been nagging at me since the boys were born. But connecting with her meant crossing an invisible line, and I wasn't sure what I would find on the other side.

That summer, I took my grandmother's letter out of the hope chest and reread it. I also reread the letters from Margaret, put them in chronological order, and wanted more. I wanted to know the whole story. I wanted to know my family. And one day, I finally did something about it. I called the Victoria Home, on impulse, while the boys were down for an afternoon nap. I called the operator for information, got the number, and dialed quickly, before I lost my nerve.

When a woman answered, I identified myself and said I was looking for my grandmother. "Her name is Mary Preston and I wonder if you know where I might find her?"

"Yes," she said. "She's standing right here. Do you want to talk to her?"

I hadn't expected this.

"No," I said. The thought of actually *talking* to my grand-mother filled me with nervous anxiety. "Just tell her that her granddaughter called." I left my number and hung up.

My grandmother had been employed at the Victoria Home, a retirement home for British Americans, for several years, but had recently moved to Chicago. She just happened to be visiting the day I called. She just happened to be standing right next to the phone.

She called back immediately. "Is this Lori?" Her British accent delighted me. "I've just been thinking of you," she said.

We were both surprised and flustered to be talking to one another, and it thrilled her to hear about the boys. "Twins!"

She said I must send her some photographs and gave me her address in Chicago. We didn't talk long. I told her I would write to her soon, and we ended our conversation.

I hung up feeling stunned. I could hardly believe I had done it. I *talked* to my grandmother. Amazing. I wrote her a letter immediately, and she wrote back—the beginning of a twenty-year correspondence.

My dear Lori,

I have just got back from New York and found a lot of letters to attend to so this is just a short note to thank you for phoning me and also writing to me and sending the lovely snaps. You look like your mother and the boys look fantastic. Very healthy and with wonderful names.

I worked in hotels for years—was five years at Victoria Home in Ossining. I am now retired and have a nice apartment in a senior citizen's building. I have so much to tell you and ask you. Where is Benny these days? Good to know Marie and Syl are well. I will come and see you as soon as I can, but since I moved in here six months ago it has been all go-go-go. Please give my love to Marie and all the folks who remember me.

All good wishes and love.
Grandma

I don't remember telling my mom that I made contact with Mary Preston, but I must have. They talked on the phone in October of 1981. My mom had probably been babysitting when my grandmother called me. And I must have come home and heard about the call, which must have been uncomfortable. But I have no memory of this.

October 19, 1981

My dear Lori,

Thank you for your letter. Sorry to have not got you on the phone, but it was nice to have a chat with your Mum. At her suggesting I will be with you on Friday October 30th. There is a train which leaves Chicago at 11:50, arriving in Kalamazoo at 3:19. I am sure I will fit in comfortably in your apartment—I am very adaptable having moved around for about fifty years. [...]

Love and all good wishes,
Grandma "P"

Whenever the subject of Mary Preston came up during conversations with my mom, I spoke with diplomatic restraint. I pretended my grandmother's visit was not a big deal, even though I felt tremendously excited about it, like anticipating a meeting with royalty or a movie star. *What would I say?*

When the passengers got off the train in Kalamazoo, I walked right past my tiny white-haired grandmother. I headed toward a tall, elegant woman in a red coat. Mary had to call my name to get my attention; she said she recognized me immediately.

"You have the Preston chin," she said.

I ushered her to my car, a crappy yellow Mazda, feeling self-conscious and hyperaware. Thankfully, my mom and Jane came to visit that weekend as well, relieving me from the pressure of being constantly "on." Jane spent the weekend in a nearby motel with our grandmother, while my mom stayed in the apartment with me, Mike, and the boys. Any worries I had about what to say were conveniently taken care of by the boys being nine months old and the stars of the show.

Terribly impressed with my cultured British grandmother and eager to be accepted by her, I exhibited my best behavior during her visit. I played at being a happy, well-adjusted person—the ideal mother, wife, daughter, hostess, and housekeeper.

November 18, 1981

Dear Lori,

Thank you for your letter and also the one from "the boys" which I appreciate very much. [...] While we were in the motel Jane asked me about her mother—but it is very difficult to tell as we lived a totally different life to the one you live here now. I sent some snaps of my visit to Michigan to my sister in London and she says you look like a mixture of Ann and Hilary. [...]

I began visiting my grandmother in Chicago as often as I could, and our bond developed quickly. She had an artfully decorated apartment in a building near the upscale neighborhood of Lincoln Park. From her sixth-floor living room window, she could see the Chicago skyline and the lights of Navy Pier at night. Although she had little money, she managed to live pretty well, including several European trips she took with funds she scrimped and saved. A little white-haired dynamo, constantly on the go, she loved the city and cultural events and complained about her elderly neighbors who did nothing but sit inside their apartments all day.

"We have such a lovely garden here, and no one goes out in it except me."

My grandmother had little to say about my mother, which disappointed me, but I didn't prod her about it. She loved to talk about books, movies, plays, and current events, so I did my best to be conversant on those topics. We talked for hours and discovered we shared the same tastes and ideas about many things.

"I didn't know," she said several times with a tone of regret.

I never asked her to explain what she meant by this phrase, but I think it meant she didn't know how alike we were, how much she would enjoy getting to know me, and how sorry she'd be that she let me go—left me in Wyandotte.

"The first time I saw a picture of you I was quite shocked," she said. "You looked so much like your mother."

Getting to know my grandmother and being recognized by familial features was an affirming experience. By knowing my grandmother I became more known to myself. And now I use her as a gauge and a guidepost, in the same way people use their parents when they say things like, "Oh God, I sound just like my mother," or "I'm becoming my mother." People usually say these things in reference to behaviors that aren't desirable but seem inevitable—like when I notice myself becoming more and more opinionated, self-involved, and judgmental.

In 1992, I told my grandmother about my interest in finding my father, and she wrote to me:

> [...] I don't quite know what to think about your search for your father. I quite understand your feelings and have been thinking quite a bit lately about my wasted life and the mess of heritage. I came from a very large family but we were never close and never showed any demonstrations of affection. And a convent education did not help. I passed this on to my children. I was a good and caring mother but undemonstrative, and we lived a strange, unconventional life. My husband was very demonstrative and great fun at times but had no sense of responsibility and was a poor provider. It was all very complicated. [...]

I eventually met my grandmother's youngest children—Hilary, David, and Timothy—each of whom suffered psychological distress as a result of being abandoned during and following World War II. Mary was not a naturally nurturing person, though she softened as she aged. She began saying "Love you" in a lilting way at the end of telephone conversations.

Born in London in 1907, Mary was educated at Catholic boarding schools. "I was sent to a convent school to be brought up as a young lady," she explained. Both of her parents were Irish. "My father was a medical student studying at Trinity College in Dublin when he met my mother. They married very young."

Mary told me this story about her parents, but it wasn't completely true. While researching family history many years later, I discovered that Mary's father didn't meet Mary's mother until *after* receiving his medical degree from Trinity. While practicing medicine in Lancashire, England, the young physician married a nineteen-year-old Irish servant who had become pregnant with his child.

"We were neither fish, nor fowl, nor good red herring." Mary occasionally made this statement in reference to her family, meaning they were of no specific economic or social class. Although her father had come from a long line of property-owning lords of the manor, the family fortune suffered during the Irish War of Independence, and her mother was a Catholic farm girl.

On one of my visits to Chicago in the late 1990s, I brought a video camera along and let it roll as my grandmother talked about her life. In this footage she sits on the floral-patterned couch in her apartment, wearing a yellow summer dress and a colorful necklace of large wooden beads. "My father was a very good man, a Quaker," she says. "He worked for the poorest of the poor. He had his own dispensary, even though that sort of thing was on the way out in the twenties."

Her father wanted her to study to be a pharmacist, but she rebelled. "I studied at the Royal College of Pharmacy and Chemistry for a year, but I was more interested in doing the Charleston. I was always hurrying off to parties and so I didn't pass my exams. But I did do a bit of dispensing. My father would pay me two and sixpence, and I could buy quite a lot with that. I could get myself a new pair of silk stockings."

Mary met John Preston on a tennis court. A flamboyant character, John did not impress Mary's family for reasons I can only guess at. One of her brothers punched John in the face and told him to *leave my sister alone!* But Mary ran off and married John when she was twenty.

When I asked why they divorced, Mary said that John had become unpredictable, cruel, and chaotic. "We didn't decide to separate. I *went*. Walked away. With no idea how to support myself or my children." She had to go out and work for the first time in her life, and she was over forty by then.

Mary talked about her struggles to make ends meet after she left her husband and spoke in defense of her actions toward her children. "I did stick with them. I tried to keep them with me and make as much of a home for them as I could." She said she didn't know what else she could have done.

If my grandmother's childbearing years had come a few decades later, I doubt she would have had so many children; she would have gone on the pill, or her husband would have had a vasectomy. She would not have neglected her children because there would not have been so many of them.

When I met my grandmother, I didn't know she had essentially abandoned her children during the war years and left the youngest alone in England when she emigrated. This might explain why she evaded answering my questions about those years. She couldn't tell me much about my mother's childhood because she wasn't *there* for so much of it. She claimed she did the best she could, but in retrospect, I wonder how her lack of involvement in her children's lives might have weighed on her.

My grandmother often remarked about my wonderful mothering skills, though I didn't agree with her assessment. Far from being the patient mother I would have liked to have been, I felt tremendous guilt about the times my nerves had frazzled and I had snapped. But Mary saw only the affection and attention I gave to my sons, so different than it had been in her day, when babies were wheeled to the back of the garden in prams and left there alone for an "airing."

For my birthday in 1983, my grandmother gave me a copy of Erma Bombeck's book of humorous essays, *Motherhood: The Second Oldest Profession*. Inside she wrote: "All good wishes to Hilary, one of the best of mothers." Beneath this, she wrote a quote from Euripides: "Oh, what a power is motherhood possessing, a potent spell. All women alike fight fiercely for the child."

Mary often recalled how she arrived in America penniless, with only a big trunk of books and a few mementos. After working as a housekeeper for a year, she moved into an apartment on Montague Street in the Brooklyn Heights neighborhood of Brooklyn. "It was very arty in those days, with a lovely promenade at the end of the road overlooking New York harbor."

During a trip to New York City with Beth, I found my grandmother's old apartment on Montague Street and walked down to the promenade with its view of lower Manhattan and the Brooklyn Bridge. I stood looking out at that iconic scene and felt so thankful to have known my grandmother.

I was the only family member there the day my grandmother died at the age of ninety-six. Her youngest son, Timothy Preston, who also lived in Chicago, was away on a camping trip and couldn't be reached, so the nursing home staff called me to come as soon as I could. I left immediately, but by the time I got there she had already gone, quietly, in her bed, alone.

"I never asked anyone for advice," she once said, "not that that's a good thing. I've made terrible mistakes. But I've done them all on my own."

At my grandmother's memorial service, I read these excerpts from the more than two hundred letters she wrote me:

> Your kitchen decorating ideas sound wonderful. I think you take after me. I have to do things to wherever I live even if it is for only a few months. Everyone admires my apartment...
>
> Last Monday I was invited to a cocktail party by the British Consul; a marvelous penthouse on the 61st floor. The views were magnificent as it was a clear night— could see for miles over lit up Chicago...
>
> I'm reading a huge book called *The Pillars of the Earth* by Ken Follett. At the same time I'm reading some very good books of short stories. Also the *New Yorker* every week so time flies, what with getting out and walking every day...
>
> Saw a lovely Italian film yesterday, also a French film I have been waiting for has just opened. We are being taken to some botanical gardens on Monday and our local zoo on Wednesday, so another week will fly by...
>
> Here is another Pre-Raphaelite card for you. I wish I could see more of you and we could do some more art

museums together. For the first time in my life I regret not being able to drive as it has prevented me from visiting you more often and seeing more of Michigan...

Well, it's a rotten day. Grey and dark so I will get into my winter woolies and go see a good Australian film. P.S. I loved the letters from the boys. They are hanging on my kitchen door...

I am taking part in a little show for our Christmas party and we are going to do the tango...

I am just off to a two hour lecture and reading by Margaret Drabble...

Just been hospitalized for five days. Had a rough two weeks and then a cardiac catheterization. But better now. Have loads of stuff to read. Bit of an effort to do much, so just a note to greet you. Always all my best and love with the half of my heart I have left. The other half rather blocked...

I went to a bag sale today and got $100 worth of really good things for $5...

You know how I told you I was not going to bother with Christmas? Well, one thing led to another and here I am decorating and having eight Russians to tea on Sunday...

Not doing much in this hot weather. There are so many things going on but I am too old to get out and really enjoy it all. I wish I did not still have this awful urge to be everywhere and see everything...

I have a new friend. Wants to get me interested in computers but I haven't the time. I sleep in the afternoon and time flies. I'm too old anyhow and have always been slow on the uptake. I am well but do not have much energy. I am being taken to the movies this afternoon to see *Chocolat*...

What do you think of the Human Genome Project? Exciting, isn't it. I remember the excitement of the double helix in 1953. A lot of the work was done at Cambridge...

It's a beautiful day, so must get out into the sunshine and to the post office. Love and all good wishes to you all. Keep happy.

Affectionately,
Grandma

CHAPTER 15

A Big Greek

I began the search for my father knowing three things about him: he had been in Las Vegas in the spring of 1954, he was an officer in the military, and he was Greek.

I learned this last fact on the day after Thanksgiving in 1983. My mom and I were sitting at her kitchen table playing Gin Rummy that day when my cousin Benny knocked at the back door. After serving in Vietnam, Benny had hit the road, disappearing for long stretches of time. It was an occasion whenever he materialized, and I hadn't seen him in several years. Wearing a cowboy shirt tucked into crisp blue jeans and sporting a neatly trimmed beard, Benny lit up the room with his cheerful goodwill. "Auntie Marie!" He kissed my mom on the cheek, then gave me a big hug and called me "cuz."

Benny and I went out to a neighborhood bar that evening and talked for a couple of hours. He had been through a marriage, a succession of relationships, and a variety of jobs that didn't work out. "But I'm on to a good thing now," he said. "Fifteen-fifty an hour to install rig-to-rig microwave links. With benefits." He had a guaranteed job waiting for him if he could just get down to Louisiana. "I gotta get my bike tuned up so I can haul ass outta' here."

Always on the verge of changing his bad luck to good, Benny possessed the faith of an optimist in spite of the hard times he had known. Our conversation turned to the past and I asked him, "Do you think your dad might know anything about my father?"

"He never talked about it much. But I think he might have known him, or at least met him once. He told me he was Greek."

"Greek?"

I had been wondering about my nationality for years, looking for myself in others, trying to guess what it might be. But I had never considered the possibility of being Greek. I didn't know anything about Greeks except that they owned a lot of restaurants. I had been to the Greektown neighborhood in Detroit a few times and enjoyed the food and the music. I loved baklava!

"Are you sure?" I asked Benny.

"I think that's what he said. Why don't we just go ask him?"

Everyone in my family knew I knew the truth about myself by then, but the topic never came up in conversation. And that was just fine with me, since it made me uncomfortable. I would have never discussed the subject with my uncle if Benny hadn't talked me into it. We drove over to see Jim Rutledge that night.

Married to his third wife, Jim had recently retired from a cement company. He sat with his legs stretched out on a worn recliner, watching TV and smoking cigarettes in his dim living room when Benny and I unexpectedly arrived.

Benny got the conversation going by asking his dad about the accident, and Jim told us about finding Margaret's watch at the side of the road.

"God damn if it wasn't her watch laying right there." He pantomimed picking the watch up as he talked. He held his hand out in front of him for a long time, as if he still held the watch, and then he repeated the story.

He told us there was a guy driving the car, but he didn't know his name. And I could hardly believe how easily this information came flowing out, readily available just for the asking. When I finally had the nerve to ask about my father, Jim said he'd heard him referred to as a big Greek. He said he didn't know my father, had never met him, and didn't know his name.

"He was a big Greek from Vegas, that's all I know."

Jim went up into his attic and brought some things to me in a manila envelope. He gave me my mother's passport, her Clark County Sheriff's Office identification card, a copy of her death certificate, and a map of the cemetery showing where she and Margaret are buried.

"I marked an X there, where the grave is," he told me. "They're in there, one on top of the other. But there isn't any marker or anything."

"Well I'll be damned," Benny said.

Our mothers were buried together in one grave.

After that night at my uncle's house, I became a slightly more complete person, a person who could say, "I am English, Irish, and Greek," a fact that delighted me. I felt grateful for what I learned from Jim Rutledge, and grateful for the items he gave me.

And yet I couldn't help wondering what happened to Ann's other possessions. There must have been personal items in her room when she died—a hairbrush, jewelry, correspondence. Maybe an address book. Things I would have cherished so much.

Search Journal: August 2006

I haven't heard anything from Jack Kogan's nephew, or the curator at the Nevada State Museum, about the picture of my mother on Fremont Street, but I have been looking at it a lot lately. I have been studying it with a magnifying glass, examining the objects in the window, the slot machines in the background, and the dark interior. I'm sure this photo must have been taken at a casino, and I keep wondering if this is where my mother worked.

While scrutinizing the photo recently, it occurred to me that my mother's employment history is probably listed in her Social Security records. So I called the Social Security Administration and asked how I would go about getting my deceased mother's record. I said I wanted it for my family history and that I just wanted to know the place of her employment in 1954.

The woman on the phone said they usually wouldn't release that information, but if I only wanted to know *where* she worked, not how much income she made, it would probably be okay. She told me I needed to go to my local Social Security office to talk to someone in person.

So I gathered up my birth certificate, my mother's birth certificate, her death certificate, the document in which I am named her beneficiary, and headed over to my local SSA office the next morning. I went dreaming of how wonderful it would be to have a specific place in Las Vegas to research, maybe even visit. But after waiting an hour to see someone, I was told a perfunctory *no*. I didn't even have a chance to show my documentation. "We can't do that," the woman at the window said with a dismissive tone.

"But I was told on the phone that I could get the information if I came here and talked to someone about it."

"Let me ask my supervisor." She got up and spoke to a guy across the room who seemed to be on his way to some other problem. I heard her say "family history," which sounded like something they get all the time and don't consider important. She came back and asked for my Social Security number. She typed it into her computer, and then asked for my name, date of birth, and birthplace. When I said San Jose she smiled and said, "I have two aunts in San Jose."

"Oh," I said and smiled back, as if this were the most fascinating thing I had heard all day. I took this pleasant exchange as a good sign.

Then she asked for my mother's name and Social Security number as she typed and looked at her screen—a screen potentially full of information about my mother. She seemed satisfied with my answers and passed a form over to me. "Just fill this out and send it in," she said. "Just follow the instructions."

"Okay. Thanks," I said, and walked away.

I didn't look at the form until I got to my car in the parking lot. I had been given a "Request for Social Security Statement." This is a form you fill out if you want a statement of your earnings history and an estimate of the benefits you'll be eligible for in the future. I didn't see how this form could possibly be of any help to me. This is a request you're only supposed to make for yourself. It requires a signature. Wouldn't it seem odd that a woman who's been dead since 1955 was requesting her earnings statement?

I sat in my car and briefly imagined storming back into the office, flinging the form through the service window, and demanding an answer to my question. But that seemed a little crazy, especially at a place with a security officer in the waiting room. And anyway, I never have the nerve to do things like that. I *avoid* confrontation.

I started my car and drove away, pissed off at bureaucracy. "Why?" I asked out loud while tightening my grip on the steering wheel. Why couldn't I have this information? It didn't make sense. It was *my* mother. I was her only child. I just wanted to know where she worked. It should not be such a big damn deal. It should not be so hard to get this simple thing!

I came home and slammed doors. I couldn't think. Couldn't relax. It took me hours to calm down, knowing this anger was about more than just the Social Security office. This anger was about being denied. It was about wanting something *so* much and not being able to have it. Something so simple. So basic. Something everyone else takes for granted.

CHAPTER 16

Benny

Things weren't going well for my cousin Benny in the summer of 2006. His wife had recently left him and the water pipes in his trailer had ruptured. Unemployed, and temporarily living with his sister, Benny had a job coming up to do some house painting. After that he planned to leave town.

"The prospect of another road trip has me chomping at the bit," he said.

Life has never been easy for Benny, but no matter the circumstances he remains upbeat. He never complains or blames. I remember him as a skinny teenager in the 1960s, a good-humored guy who wore horn-rimmed glasses, talked in silly voices, and seemed to know something about everything. He loved to recite facts and explain things, which is probably why the adults considered him a pest. But I didn't know anyone else like Benny, and admired him for being funny and smart.

Benny met his first wife on the West Coast in the 1970s, and brought her home to meet the family during one of his rare appearances. We gathered together at Uncle Jim's house to greet the newlyweds, and what I remember about that day is Benny roughhousing with Jane's sons in the living room. I remember him standing there, flush from the activity, saying he looked forward to having a couple of "rug rats" of his own someday.

I had never heard this phrase before, which might be why the memory of that moment sticks with me, but I also remember Benny's hopeful attitude when he said it. I'm sure he would have welcomed the opportunity to be a regular guy: a husband and father with a dependable, steady job. But things never worked out that way for him.

After reconnecting in the early 1980s, Benny and I began writing letters to each other. In May of 1985, he wrote me this letter from Slidell, Louisiana:

Hello "cuz"

Good to hear from you! I just got back here. Got your letter as I pulled in the driveway. Last Sunday I hitched to Riverview, got my bike fixed and hit the road. Got a ticket in Ohio for following too close and then in Dayton, lost my damn chain.

Spent Thursday night at a Days Inn with a biker out of Detroit. He had a Gold Wing Interstate and just cruised along, with me blowin' like a rag doll off my handle bars. I could hear his stereo over the wind screammmmm. So he sprung for a double at the Days Inn 'bout 2:30 a.m. I knew that fat boy was queer as purple peas, but I was tired! No problem, but when I got up he was sitting on his bed with a map, facing me, sound asleep. Weird?

So ya just flipped off old Mike and split? Gad Zooks! I know, believe me, I know where you're at. I wish you all the best at being a new "single parent." I know you're going thru hard personal and emotional times, so hang tight girl, and not on the first guy you meet either!

I love ya,
Your cuz, Ben

I visited Benny while he was staying at Jane's during the summer of 2006, and he appeared untroubled in spite of his hardships. Jane, however, was fed up. "He sabotages himself," she complained to me. "He can't keep a job because he's smarter than everybody else, you know?"

Benny seems to take after our eccentric Preston relatives, while Jane has always been down-to-earth, like her father. Even though they were in their fifties in the summer of 2006, Benny and Jane reminded me of their teenage selves. They both still told corny jokes, and punctuated their speech with high-pitched exclamatory sounds.

Jane was on her bus route when I sat down to talk to Benny. I told him I was writing about our family and wanted to know what he remembered about the past. I asked him if he knew where the old photo albums were.

"They're right here." He pulled one of the albums out from a stack of newspapers and magazines on an end table. "We were just looking at them the other night."

I cringed at the casual treatment of the photo albums, our Rosetta stones. Benny carried the album to the dining room table and I joined him there as he flipped through the pages.

"It was important for Dad to get Margaret into the States before I was born so I could be a citizen," he said while looking at a photo of himself, a newborn in his mother's arms.

Benny always refers to his mother as *Margaret*, never as "my mother."

He crossed the room to rummage around in a box of his belongings and came back with Margaret's "Transoceanic Flight Certificate"—a souvenir of her trip to the United States. He handed it to me, and I held it with wonder. It amazed me that Benny still possessed this item and knew right where to find it in spite of all the moving around he'd done.

Margaret arrived in the United States in October of 1948 and went to stay with her mother-in-law, our Grandma Rutledge, while Jim took part in the Berlin Airlift. "The Navy led off with planes out of Oakland and Honolulu, taking supplies to Germany," Benny explained. "Dad's squadron became the

Military Air Transport Service, known as MATS." He would have gladly launched into a lecture of military history, but I pulled him back to the story.

"So, your mother joined your dad in California after you were born?"

"Yep. Grandma Rutledge hired a soldier to ride on the train with Margaret to make sure she wouldn't ditch me."

"What?" I stared at Benny in disbelief. I had never heard this story.

"She paid the guy twenty bucks."

"That's crazy. Why would she do that? " I asked.

"Margaret hated being pregnant. She hated having a child. She was only eighteen and here she was, finally free of that big family of hers, spreading her wings, but now she's got this *kid*."

It disturbed me to hear Benny say this. "Oh, no," I told him. "I don't think it was like that at all. Your mother *loved* you."

"It was a three-day train ride and Grandma was genuinely concerned that Margaret would abandon me," Benny insisted.

"Well, just because Grandma was concerned doesn't make her concern *valid*. Grandma probably just didn't understand your mother. You have to consider how different they were, what different cultures they came from."

Louise Rutledge, a poor, uneducated, cheerless woman, must have been shocked that her son married a girl from England. A foreigner with an accent. A *pregnant* foreigner. I doubt she had a warm or comfortable relationship with Margaret.

I told Benny I couldn't believe his mother wasn't happy to have him.

"Just look at these pictures," I said. Page after page of the album on the table before us displayed photos of a happy-looking Margaret with her baby boy.

"I know," Benny said. "That's the irony of it. But when Grandma said that to me..."

He stopped talking and looked off in the distance.

"Well, I think it's strange that she even told you that story. I think it was *mean*."

Benny shrugged it off. "Anyway," he said, "Margaret made the trip to Oakland and joined up with Dad. I still have the pack of Union Pacific playing cards she got on the train."

He flipped a page and I thought, again, of how unfortunate it was that Benny and Jane were never shown these photo albums when they were kids. How could their father have left them in an attic all those years? All those years when Benny went around with a grief for his mother he probably never expressed and the belief that she didn't want him.

I asked Benny what he remembered about Margaret.

"The only memory I have is of her saying, 'There's a giraffe coming in under the door.' I thought that was so *funny*. Of course she'd said 'draft,' but I was a little boy and I just wondered how a giraffe could squeeze under the door. It's impossible!"

I asked what else he remembered about Margaret and he said, "That's it."

He looked intently at a picture of his mother on Waikiki beach as he told me this, and I asked what he remembered about Hawaii.

"I remember getting there," he said.

What seems most memorable to Benny about his early years are the airplanes. "We flew to Hawaii on a seaplane. A huge Martin Mars. A flying boat." Benny lived in Hawaii as a toddler, and then returned after the accident. "Dad made his model airplane there. A Lockheed Constellation that he got in a kit from Japan."

"So you had just turned six when the accident happened..."

"Was I that old? Huh. I guess so. All I remember is Dad coming in to me and Jane and saying, 'Your mother isn't coming home anymore.' You know he always had that particular aroma about him of Old Spice and cigarettes. And a scratchy beard."

"And then your dad married Carol."

"Yep. His old high school sweetheart. She came to live with us in Hawaii."

There is a picture of Jim, Carol, Benny, and Jane. They are standing in front of a naval ship. Carol is loaded with leis; Benny and Jane are in their Sunday best. Jim has his arm around Carol, but there is a distance between the adults and the kids.

Benny never had an easy relationship with his stepmother, but he never expressed any animosity toward her. "She hated us kids," he said and then laughed. He changed the subject. "We lived in Quonset huts. I remember raiding the neighbors' gardens for hibiscus and gardenias to make leis. And there was so much fruit. Pineapple, papaya, mango. They'd fill a big crystal bowl with fruit and doctor it up with rum for card parties."

Benny sent me an e-mail that fall. He had gone back down to Louisiana again and wrote to me from a library computer.

[...] I am now working at the EZ-PAY Tire in Slidell. Doing mostly maintenance right now. The boss is letting me sleep in a 24' motor home on the tire store property. Pretty nice, as opposed to sleeping in the Honda. It's got A/C, electricity, shower, and a refrigerator. The Honda barely made it this time; the thermostat went haywire 400 miles from Slidell. I had to stop every 100 miles and feed it water. [...] The Social Security people said I am qualified for limited disability due to bone spurs on my spine. I will receive cash and Medicare/Medicaid etc. Weather is in the 90s and very sunny.

CHAPTER 17

A Terrible Thing to Lose

M ike and I were divorced and I had gone back to college when I met Tim Harper, a tall, handsome carpenter. Tim designed his own house, which he was in the process of building when we met. Constructed on a wooded plot of land thirty minutes from Kalamazoo, the house had cedar siding, a wood stove, and plans for a large deck that never actually materialized.

We fell in love and we were a good match in many respects, except for the incompatibilities we ignored, the way people in love tend to do. In spite of being a bona fide city girl, I romantically believed I could adapt to country life. I moved into Tim's house when my sons were ten and the house was *almost* complete. We had a small wedding, and I found a job at a nearby branch of the district library.

Located in a rural village, the library had oak shelves built by the WPA in the 1930s and two big windows that looked out onto the main street. I loved the library, but the village was dismal. When I drove my grandmother over to see it during one of her visits she said, "Well. This is a soul-destroying place."

I was not fond of the locale, but enjoyed my work. For eight years I read storybooks to preschoolers, hunted for answers to reference questions, created cheery window displays, and prided myself on always knowing just the right book to recommend to my regular patrons.

One dull day at the library, I typed "Air Force 1954" into the recently installed computer. Our built-in card catalog had become a thing of the past, and I felt sorry about that. I had enjoyed the precise method of filing catalog cards, sliding the long, narrow drawers in and out of their slots. But I adapted quickly to the computer. "Air Force 1954" might have been my first personal search query.

Google didn't exist yet, but we were hooked up to some library databases. My query led to a government publication called the *Air Force Register*, an annual list of Air Force officers, published from 1951 to 1968. It thrilled me to realize my father's name would most likely be listed in the 1954 edition. *My father's name!*

The nearest library with the register in their catalog was in Grand Rapids—an hour's drive north. And since the register could not be loaned out, I drove to Grand Rapids and spent a Saturday afternoon there. I located the 1954 edition of the register, a document that listed 23,127 names, and carefully went through it, page by page. Mistakenly believing my father's name to be Stanley, I found more than seventy men with that name and copied them into a spiral notebook. This notebook became the basis of my search for the next few years, but I had no luck finding a Greek Air Force officer named Stanley.

When I began to search again in 2006, I counted on getting rosters from Nellis and Fallon via the Freedom of Information Act requests I had made. But as hope of actually receiving those rosters diminished, I decided to take another look at the *Air Force Register*. I drove over to the library—just ten minutes from my house since I lived in Grand Rapids then—and expected the register to be waiting for me on the shelf where I left it nearly ten years earlier. But I couldn't find it.

"Sorry," the librarian said after looking for it on her computer.

This caused me to physically slump.

I had come to the library anticipating the pleasure of having some actual names to investigate. Instead I suddenly felt fed up with the whole endeavor. I went over to an upholstered chair near a window, sat down, and doodled dejectedly on the fresh yellow legal pad I had brought along—a pad I had expected to fill with names and information.

I'll never find him, I thought while fighting back tears and feeling foolish.

I moped around for a couple of days after that. Then I stumbled upon the website of an organization called the Sabre Pilots Association. I learned that the F-86 Sabre Jet had been the primary Air Force fighter aircraft used during the Korean War, and many Sabre Jet pilots were trained at Nellis Air Force Base from 1951 to 1955.

"The best damn pilots that ever stepped into a cockpit," the website proclaimed.

The Saber Pilots Association had more than eight hundred members and held a reunion in Las Vegas every two years. The next one was scheduled for May of 2007—a gathering of men that might include my father.

Searching with renewed determination, I learned that copies of the *Air Force Register* were held at the Detroit Public Library and Indiana State University. Armed with this information, I approached my local reference librarian again. I wanted to know if the 1954 edition of the register could be borrowed from these other libraries.

She did a little keyboard clicking and said, "It's only available on microfiche in Detroit, and I'm not sure that Indiana would loan it out."

I told her I'd consider *driving* to Indiana to look at this book if I knew for certain the 1954 edition was there. This seemed to pique her interest. She sat up straight and brushed some lunch crumbs off her blouse. She decided to take a quick trip down to the special collections department in the library's basement while I waited.

In minutes, the librarian returned. She plopped the book in front of me like a hunter returning with meat. There it was: *Air Force Register 1954*. I sat still for a moment and just looked at the thick green paperbound document.

"Thank you," I said.

"Sure," she said. "Do you want to check it out?"

I was going to be able to take the register home and search through it at my leisure. *Wow.* I walked out of the library with a grin on my face and the register clutched to my chest. It felt like my lucky day. The document in my hands contained 23,127 names, and I felt certain one of them belonged to my father.

I returned home in a happy, hopeful mood and immediately got to work. I decided to comb through the register and copy out every Greek-sounding name, which were not hard to find since almost all Greek surnames end with an s—Bourikas, Giannakos, Kokkinos, etc.

I soon came upon the name Demetrios Elipoulos, which sounded especially Greek to me. I Googled Mr. Elipoulos and learned he had been a bomber pilot during World War II. He was stationed in England, and while returning from a bombing mission to Germany one night, his plane was shot down over occupied France. He survived, made his way to a farmhouse, and with the help of the French Resistance managed to make his way back to England. I found versions of this dramatic story on three separate sites, including one that mentioned his wife and three sons. *My potential half-brothers?*

After the war, Demetrios continued his Air Force career until his retirement in 1970. His career included training pilots, though where he did this training wasn't mentioned. I found photos of him as a young pilot, and also one of him taken in 2004 in which he has a head full of white hair and striking dark eyes. I became obsessed with these photos. It astounded me to look at his face and think, *this could be him.*

I looked him up in an online telephone directory and found him listed in Santa Barbara, California. Then I looked up a lot of other Elipouloses—my possible siblings and cousins. I printed everything I could find, and the more I read the more convinced I became. I could easily imagine my mother hooking up with a guy who had been in England during the war, a guy who trained pilots, just as her father had. It also seemed likely that a distinctive name like Demetrios Elipoulos might have been why Jim Rutledge remembered him as a Greek.

I could hardly think or talk about anything other than Demetrios for days after discovering him. I stayed up late at night, searching online for potential relatives and taking every little similarity as a sign. I found an Eliopoulos who worked in theater, another who was a photographer. Then I couldn't sleep, I couldn't wind down. In the shower I had trouble remembering if I had just washed my hair or not.

Handsome, intelligent, and successful, Demetrios fulfilled all the hopes I had for my father. When I looked at his face and thought of him *as* my father, it gave me an idea of what it would be like to actually know. Not only would I finally be whole, I would also be defined in the context of having come from this man and his family. This family would substantiate my worth.

I assumed that Demetrios had been at Nellis at some point in his military career since the F-86 appeared on the list of aircraft he piloted. But I didn't know if he had been there at the same time my mother lived in Las Vegas. I needed an answer to that pivotal question, and I had Demetrios's phone number, just not the nerve to actually call him.

I had to ask Beth for her help, despite the dismay my obsession caused her. The more I talked about Demetrios, the less she wanted to hear. We were living in the same house, but we were in completely different places. Beth dwelled with the constant worry of finding a new job, while I flew around on the fantasy of finding my father. I could not have picked a worse time to be obsessed with anything other than our financial security. Even though Beth received a generous severance and her prospects were good, I'm sure she would have rather seen me searching the want ads than scouring the web for Elipouloses.

I had to cajole her into it, but Beth said *okay*, she'd help. So we plotted it out. She would call Demetrios and tell him she had an uncle about to celebrate his eightieth birthday. We would make up a name for this fictitious uncle, and Beth would say she was looking for men who had known him in his Air Force days. She would say her uncle had been at Nellis in 1954 and ask Demetrios if he had been there at the same time.

We ran through all the possible ways Demetrios could respond and rehearsed what Beth would say in each case. When we were sure we had our story straight, Beth sat at our dining room table with a script laid out in front of her as I paced around in the kitchen. She dialed his number, introduced herself, and told him our story, to which Demetrios replied, "Oh, well, that was long after I was gone, I was there in '50." And the conversation ended.

Beth thanked him for his time, said goodbye, and hung up. My high hopes fizzled, and I fell back to earth with a thud. I sat on a kitchen chair, utterly dejected. But not completely convinced. "Just because he wasn't stationed at Nellis in 1954 doesn't mean he wasn't in *Vegas* at that time," I said.

Beth shook her head. "You have to accept the fact that this man is not your father." She encouraged me to let it go, but I wasn't ready to do that. I did not cross Demetrios off my list. I made a plan to call him again myself, after some time went by, and ask him directly about my mother. *What did I have to lose?*

Beth went back into our home office, back to the job hunt or another game of computer solitaire, and I returned to the search. I sat at our dining room table and tried to shake off the loss. I tried to go back to the task of searching for Greek names in the register but couldn't concentrate. I sat there with those pages and pages of names before me and felt a physical stab of pain. Like heartbreak. Like grief.

I closed the register, shoved it across the table, got up, and went out into our backyard. I crossed our brick patio and opened the side door of our 1930s-era garage. I went inside, shut the door, and stood weeping among our rakes and shovels and bags of mulch, feeling as miserably bereaved as I have ever been.

Demetrios had personified my father. He had made my unknown father seem tangible. *Possible.* He was a real man with a name, a face, and a family—the kind of family I would be proud to be part of. And that was a terrible thing to lose. I felt sad and weepy for several days afterward, and it seemed crazy to have brought this grief on myself. I felt like a fool to have so easily believed, to have been flying so high. So sure.

CHAPTER 18

A Foreign Word

"Where is your birth certificate?"

I had recently turned sixteen, and we were getting ready to go apply for my driver's license. "I'll get it," I said.

Sometime during my early teens, I had taken the baby book from my mom's closet and hidden it in mine, along with all the old letters and photographs. My birth certificate, tucked into the baby book, had been folded in half and then unfolded and refolded every time I took a look at it. It had grown soft and tattered.

My mom must have been aware that I had removed the baby book from her closet, but she never said a word to me about it. She never mentioned the baby book, the letters, or the photographs, and neither did I.

I retrieved the birth certificate from my room and put it in my pocket while my mom waited impatiently, car keys in hand.

"You got it?"

"Yeah." I answered with the annoyed tone of a teenager, and off we went.

At the driver's license bureau, I wrote my name on the application: *Hilary Ann Bocianowski.* When I handed it over, along with my birth certificate, which had the name Hilary Ann *Preston* on it, the woman behind the counter furrowed her brow. She looked at my mom and asked, "Is she adopted?"

"No," my mom said. A statement that floored me. Until that moment, I'd assumed my parents had legally adopted me. I stared at my mom, but she did not look back.

"Well, I can't issue her a license like this."

My heart sank.

"I can issue her license as Hilary Preston, or you can see about having her name changed." The woman behind the counter looked from my mom to me. *I wanted my license!* It would have been fine with me if the name on it were Hilary Preston, but I stood mute, and my mom did not look happy. She put her purse up on the counter and exhaled.

"How would we go about that?" she asked.

It took more than a year before I finally got my license. I had to go to court and legally change my name, a process I experienced as an embarrassment. I had to answer in court that I wanted my name to be Bocianowski, a name the judge had trouble pronouncing. I ended up with a document which lists my "aka"— also known as—name. I became Hilary Ann Bocianowski, also known as Hilary Ann Preston. Though none of my friends or family called me Hilary.

When I married Mike, I became Lori Reilly, a person I now hardly recognize as having been me when I look at photographs or read old diaries. When Mike and I divorced, I decided to leave my Lori identity behind. I introduced myself to new people as Hilary and asked those who called me Lori to stop, including my therapist, a wise woman who found the switch in name significant.

It took some time, but everyone I knew made the transition—everyone except my mom and my cousins. They never called me Hilary without sounding as if they were mocking me. They said "Hilary" in a way that implied pretentiousness, as if I were trying to be someone I was not, instead of the exact opposite.

When I married Tim, I became Hilary Harper, a name I am happy with and plan to keep. I used to joke that I married Tim just for the alliterative name. We lived together until 1999, the year my sons graduated from high school, and also the year in which I came to realize my interest in women wasn't a fluke or a passing phase.

How could I not have known this important thing about myself?

At the age of thirteen or fourteen, I had an experience with a girl from my neighborhood, an incident for which I have only an abbreviated memory. I can't recall the specific circumstances, but I remember being in a bed with this girl, kissing and touching. I remember the arousal, the thrill—my first sex. But I only remember snippets of this experience due to the shame it caused. I deliberately worked to forget it. Whenever a memory of it popped into my brain, I immediately thought of something else, and in this way managed to repress it.

I had almost completely forgotten the incident until my twenties, when I had a few more brief "experiences." There was a particularly memorable make-out session in the bathroom stall of a bar. And another on a camping trip. Women undoubtedly aroused me.

I had read the lesbian section of *Our Bodies Ourselves* with much interest. Several times. But it didn't dawn on me that all of this might *mean* something. I kept on wishing for the ideal guy to come along—the guy who would save me. Define me. Prove me worthy, and make me whole. I did not set out to deny my attraction to women, I just didn't take it seriously. My desire for women did not seem as significant as the approval and love I desired from men.

The last few years I spent with Tim were difficult and emotional. My involvement with a community theater group in the town of Paw Paw, a twenty-minute drive from our home in the woods, kept me busy and boosted my mood. I would become intensely engaged during the rehearsal and production period of a show, neglecting my family and my job. And then crash and burn when it was all over.

When I did finally fall in love with a woman, it was with an emotionally unavailable woman, resulting in a long, dreary time of romantic obsession and torment. I would delete this period of my life if I could. I would like to click "undo," especially since this occurred while my sons were teenagers. I regret not being fully present for them for several years. I am sorry about being so sad sometimes it must have disturbed them, and so giddy at times I behaved like a teenager myself.

I'm just glad my mom wasn't around for any of this. I can't imagine what it would have been like to come out to Marie, although I'm sorry she wasn't there to see the boys grow up. She died in January of 1994, two months after her seventieth birthday. My dad found her, dead, on the floor next to her bed.

He called me at five in the morning—the one and only phone call my dad ever made to me. My mom had taped my number up on the wall next to the phone in case of emergency. "LORI" she had written large with a permanent marker.

My dad very rarely made phone calls. When he absolutely had to talk to someone, my mom would dial for him. It would be a big deal, with all the drama of looking up the number in the phone book and making sure it was the right one. "Pytlewski! Pete! On Chestnut!" he'd be shouting, exasperated by the process.

The phone ringing woke us up. When Tim handed the receiver to me and said, "It's your dad," I had a dreadful feeling.

"Ma's dead."

"No." I experienced instant denial. This could not be so. I had just talked to her the day before. She said she felt pretty good. She had plans to go to bingo.

It took more than a year before I could look at a picture of my mom without crying. She died in the middle of a long, hard winter with record amounts of snow. The week after her funeral, we were snowed in. Everything closed, including the library where I worked. Grieving and going stir-crazy, I let out a sound one afternoon, a loud moaning wail. I held onto the sink for support and just let it out, which was a good thing for me, but undoubtedly unnerving for my sons in the next room.

After my mom's death, I felt angry at her for leaving me alone with my dad. His health had declined, and I wished he would not live much longer—a wish I had a hard time expressing. My friends did not relate. They expected me to possess some shred of daughterly regard for this man, but I did not. People spoke of their fathers in ways I could not comprehend. "Father" was a foreign word to me, a word from a lost language, impossible to decipher or pronounce.

There is not one good thing my dad ever said to me or did for me, and I have a hard time remembering anything likeable or admirable about him. I have to try really hard to come up with this: He loved my sons. He grew good tomatoes. And I liked going for rides in his fishing boat, fast on the river, when I was a kid. That's it.

When my dad died a few years after my mom, I graciously accepted condolences from visitors at the funeral home. Solemn and polite, I greeted relatives I hadn't seen since my mom's burial and would most likely never see again. The funeral process took three long days and concluded with a luncheon at the Dom Polski Hall. My cousins arranged the details. A buffet table had been set up with more than enough kielbasa, stuffed cabbage, and mashed potatoes for the handful who lingered without much to say.

Tim and my sons left early in order to be back home in time for a middle school basketball game, so I was on my own after the last relative departed. I drove to the house on Cedar Street feeling relieved that it was all over. I felt free. Unburdened. I unlocked the back door, walked into the kitchen, and just stood still for a few moments. Then I went into the dining room where I tugged on the window shades, letting them fly up and rattle around, disturbing layers of long-settled dust.

I had been looking forward to doing this, and I wasn't disappointed as the room filled with an uncustomary brightness. I went from room to room then, opening curtains, pulling up shades, pushing up windows—bringing life into this house that had so long suffered from a lack of adequate air and light. I went out onto the enclosed front porch and undid all the locks and latches. I turned on the radio. I tuned in some old Motown.

My dad died in March of 1999. That fall I took a leave of absence from my job at the library to clean out the house before selling it to the city. The factory across the street had been razed, and the city was buying up the surrounding properties. They were tearing everything down, my whole block, and putting up big brick houses with master suites, mud rooms, and granite countertops, which seemed absurd to me. The new houses looked odd in my old Wyandotte neighborhood, but buyers were snatching them up as quickly as they could be built.

It took a lot less time than I expected to clear the house of its contents. I filled bag after bag for the trash or the Goodwill, arranged to have most of the furniture picked up and taken away, and then lived in the house by myself for several days of pleasant solitude, with only the sleeper sofa, kitchen table, and one chair.

Empty, the house seemed like a different place. No longer defined by its contents, the house had charm, and I realized, to my surprise, that I would miss it. I felt sad to know it would no longer exist. I thought of how everything would be shut off—the electricity, the water, the gas—all the lifelines cut. I pictured the wrecking ball crashing into it, smashing into the living room: the sudden, fatal blow. I imagined everything crumbling and falling in on itself, tumbling into the basement. The house would be a pile of rubble, and it would be my fault because I had let it go. Probably for less than I could have gotten. The city made an offer and I took it, without the heart to negotiate. I just wanted it to be done. To take the money and run.

During my last moments in the house, I stood in the middle of the living room and took a photograph: an image of the door to the porch standing open, a patch of light coming in. And then I lingered there, torn between feelings of loss and emancipation.

I had walked through every room, pulled down the shades, and taken the old phone off the wall in the dining room. I had only to sign my name and hand over the keys at city hall, but there was my mom at the kitchen table. She sat reading the paper and smoking a cigarette while something simmered on the stove.

Then here was my twelve-year-old self, dancing along to *American Bandstand*, and I knew the house would indelibly exist for me, vivid in memory, the way childhood homes remain, forever a part of who we are.

CHAPTER 19

Hilary

There is a photograph in which I am standing in front of the Cedar Street house in 1958 with Aunt Hilary. I have a scowl on my face for some reason, but she is smiling and holding my hand. In spite of being only three at the time, I vaguely remember how strange Hilary's English accent sounded, and I have a min-iscule memory of her sitting on a chair in our kitchen, a memory that stuck with me in a hazy, mysteriously significant way.

I didn't see Hilary again until she came to Kalamazoo for a visit in 1984, and I briefly visited her in Florida in 1992, but we didn't really get to know one another until after my grandmother died. I shared a hotel room with Hilary for two days while we were both in Chicago for Mary Preston's memorial service.

Several people eulogized my grandmother, including me, and Hilary said it seemed as if she didn't know the woman we spoke of. Hilary had a friendly relationship with her mother as an adult, but hadn't felt valued or loved as child. She told me about spend-ing the war years away from her parents. "It was terribly lonely," she said. "At the end of the war I was living in a convent, so I didn't get to celebrate. I wish I could have been in London."

When her family reunited after the war, her parents' relationship deteriorated. Then her mother vanished for several months. "She took off. Just disappeared," Hilary said. "And I pretty much took care of myself then. I got myself up for school every day, made my own meals."

Aunt Hilary told me about falling out of an apple tree one day in London during her mother's absence. She fell into a neighbor's yard and they called an ambulance, which she considered "very kind." Her father brought her a stuffed animal and a basket of fruit at the hospital. "Wow," she said, "I thought that was *really* nice." Margaret and Ann also came to visit at the hospital. They ate all the fruit because Hilary had injured her jaw and couldn't chew.

While telling me this story, Aunt Hilary mentioned that my mother had sometimes been called "Saint Ann" because of her perpetually good behavior. She also told me that my mother wrote a letter during her pregnancy, saying she didn't like the idea of Jim's sister adopting her baby. "I've often felt bad about that," Hilary said. "I should have fought for custody of you."

Hilary was fourteen when her mother announced, "You're going to Ireland." Sent to live with her Aunt Stella, Hilary remembers getting sick on the boat that took her across the sea and being surprised that no one met her when she arrived. She had to take a train to her Aunt Stella's house, where she found she was expected to do the housework. On her fifteenth birthday she was sent back to England and went to work as a nanny. "That was the end of my childhood."

In 1955, Aunt Hilary worked in Paris as an au pair and fell in love. "A love crisis," she called it. While the mother of the child she cared for was hospitalized with TB, she fell in love with the father. "He took me all around, showed me Paris. It was wonderful, but then the wife came back and it was terrible. I had to leave."

After immigrating to the United States, Hilary met and married a man named Sam, whom my grandmother once described as mean and alcoholic.

"Oh yes, we had some hard times," Hilary told me, "but I did love him. I was sad when he died. I still miss him."

SEP · 59

She and Sam never had children. They spent the 1960s and '70s working in Manhattan and living in Brooklyn. Sam was a cook, and Hilary worked in hotels. They worked until the 1980s and then bought some land in Florida, where they retired.

A quiet, simple, humble person, unlike her mother and her more extroverted siblings, Hilary lives in a shabby trailer in the middle of Florida with her beloved pets. She has a little nook in her kitchen where she spends most of her time. She naps, listens to the radio, and watches TV. A creature of routine, she takes her tea, her pills, and the news from the BBC at the same time every day. So it surprised me when I learned she planned to take a cross-county journey in the fall of 2006. Aunt Hilary came to visit me in Grand Rapids that fall on the first leg of a trip she took to Glacier National Park, Yellowstone, and the Grand Canyon— places she always wanted to see.

"It'll be my last trip," she told me.

At the age of seventy-one, she traveled across the country by herself in a van she had leased and loaded with camping gear. She plotted a route that took her up through Michigan and across the northern edge of the country, into the wide-open spaces of the West.

Aunt Hilary impressed me, going on that trip by herself. But the impulse to hit the road seems to run in our family. There are many wanderers among the Prestons, like my grandparents who went from place to place in the 1930s, or my cousin Benny, and my uncle Tim, both of whom traveled around the country on motorcycles. I recognize myself in these vagabonds. I like to attribute my wanderlust to genetics, even though I know it is a common yearning. I dream of driving the back roads, the "blue" highways, without a destination, for an unlimited amount of time. Just me and my camera. *Wouldn't that be the life?*

Aunt Hilary doesn't write letters, but we exchange greeting cards and phone calls several times a year. She filed for bankruptcy after her cross-country road trip. She had charged all her expenses on a credit card with no idea how she would pay it back. "I always knew it would happen someday," she said about the bankruptcy. "But it's such a lot of trouble, so much paperwork."

She didn't have a car for a while, which concerned me, considering how far out in the boonies she lives. But then she somehow managed to buy a nice new motor scooter which she got around on for a couple of years. I have tried to talk her into moving into senior-citizens' housing in a city near her, but she won't budge. When I call, she is most often in the middle of watching a classic movie, or on her way out for a walk with her dog. There is a nature preserve near her with hiking trails she enjoys. I know she's lonely, but she values her independence, and seems content with the simple pleasures of life – traits which I admire so much.

Search Journal: September 21, 2006

I went to a writing conference last weekend and paid extra to have a published author critique a sample of my work. In my introductory letter to him, I described my writing as "a memoir about being raised in a family that was not my own and not being told the truth."

He underlined this sentence and pointed it out to me at the beginning of our session. "I don't think you should write about this," he said. He explained that he had recently adopted a baby and would be hurt if his son ever said to him, "You're not my father."

"I doubt that will ever happen," I said. I told him adoptees usually want to protect their loyalty to their adoptive parents. But he wouldn't hear me. He told me again that this memoir is something I should not write.

"Maybe your mother was a prostitute and that's why she didn't know who your father was," he said.

Stunned by this, I just sat there. Speechless.

I listened to his suggestions, thanked him politely, and went away seething. As usual, I avoided conflict. I didn't respond to him with the outrage I felt, or at least some righteous indignation, as I should have. Instead, I thanked him. *Thanked him!* What is wrong with me? And what is wrong with a man who could say something so offensive to a stranger?

October 8, 2006

I finally finished reading every name in the *Air Force Register* and copied out 112 possibilities, of which twenty are Greek for sure. I am now in the process of looking for their phone numbers and calling as many as I can. When someone answers, I tell them

I'm doing genealogical research. I say I'm looking for a man who served in the Air Force, and ask if the man in question might have been stationed at Nellis or in Las Vegas for any reason in the early 1950s.

I have been getting a lot of answering machines and disconnected numbers. A lot of these men have died. I end up talking to their wives or children, who don't always know the answers to my questions and are suspicious of my motives.

One guy who had not been at Nellis said, "I wasn't one of those hot-rod flyboys."

October 12, 2006

Benny called tonight in a talkative mood. He sounded upbeat, in spite of the fact that he got fired from his job at the tire store two weeks ago. They took him off the payroll, but he's still making a couple of bucks doing maintenance and odd jobs.

He has been put out of the RV and is currently residing in the tire-store office while he waits to move into a Hurricane Katrina–damaged house. The house has been rehabbed, he explained to me, but it's not completely done. "It's had all the drywall replaced, but it doesn't have electricity, carpeting, or cabinets yet."

It will be Benny's job to finish the inside work, and his ex-wife, Belinda, plans to drive down to Louisiana and move into this house with him, to help. "We need each other," he said. Benny seems to be feeling positive about his future. He has joined the VFW, and he doesn't seem too concerned about the blackouts he's been having due to a blocked carotid artery. He said he had a medical appointment coming up at the VA, and he seemed pretty pleased about that.

October 17, 2006

It suddenly hits me: *I'm not gonna find him.*

It hits me, not like a ton of bricks, but more like a firm nudge. As if someone were trying to rouse me from a deep sleep. *Wake up and smell the coffee!*

I have lost my enthusiasm for the search. I haven't the energy to make any more calls. It seems so pointless, and I don't have the heart for it. Not today anyway, not this grey October day. It's been seven months since I began this journey, and six since Beth lost her job. *Six months!* I should be looking for a job myself instead of wasting time on this search that will likely lead nowhere.

October 26, 2006

Beth and I have begun to talk about selling the house. We have been making a list of all the things we will have to do before putting it on the market. A decidedly unhappy task. I have to force myself to keep making phone calls. Even though the next call could potentially be *the* one, I hate asking the same personal, nerve-wracking questions over and over. But I've got to finish what I began or this has all been a waste of time.

I've started sending follow-up letters to all the inconclusive possibilities. I thank them for taking the time to talk to me, ask them to contact me if they know anyone who might fit the description of the man I'm looking for, and include photos of myself and my sons.

I have also finally mailed a letter to Danielle Grise, the woman in *People* magazine. I sent her a picture of myself taken at the time her picture appeared in *People*, and also a recent photo. I explained the situation and asked her to please get in touch.

November 10, 2006

I have lost my momentum and something in me has changed, but I'm not sure what or why. I wonder if this bout of searching has simply run its course. Maybe it's like a fever that has suddenly broken. Or maybe I've just finally gotten the story out of my system.

My close call with Demetrios changed things. The grief I felt at the loss of Demetrios was sharp and strong. And maybe that's it: maybe I've finally grieved. Or maybe I'm depressed. I can't quite see things clearly. I really don't know. The weather changed today. It's winter. My bones ache. I'm content to do nothing.

December 2, 2006

The phone rang this afternoon while I pulled laundry out of the dryer in our basement. I answered on an old wall phone down there that doesn't have caller ID, and when I heard an East Coast accent I assumed it was a telemarketer of some sort. I prepared to give a swift brush-off, then realized the voice belonged to Danielle Grise. The woman in *People* magazine!

I hardly knew what to say. As it turns out, *People* never forwarded the letter I wrote to her in 1993, so my recent contact was the first she had heard of our resemblance—which she agreed was striking. During our conversation I learned that Danielle is part Greek! Her mother is Greek and English, so we have the same ethnic makeup. She said she didn't know if any of her relatives were in the Air Force but she would check it out and let me know if she comes up with anything.

I felt so astonished to actually be talking to this woman that I forgot to ask her some important questions, including her mother's maiden name. I'd like to know if it matches any of the names on my call list. But even if Danielle isn't a relative, I now feel certain of my Greek ethnicity.

December 8, 2006
Beth has been offered a job with Detroit's utility company, DTE, which is wonderful news, but I can hardly believe the location—the job would require Beth to spend part of her time at a power plant near Wyandotte. *Of all places.*

She had her final interview for this job two days ago, and I went along for the ride. We stayed the night in a hotel and made a mini-vacation out of it. The following day we took a tour of the Ford Rouge Plant, the massive industrial complex I grew up near but had never actually seen. We were standing on a viewing platform above an assembly line when Beth's cell phone rang with the news: she got the job! This news caused mixed emotions for both of us. Beth's eyes welled with tears, and I wasn't sure if they came from joy or sorrow. This job will mean selling our house in Grand Rapids and leaving behind our family and friends. We took a drive into Wyandotte that afternoon. We took a look at the river and my old neighborhood, and I enjoyed reminiscing. But I can't imagine going back.

December 25, 2006
Beth woke up this Christmas morning with an epiphany. She had a dream in which she learned the definition of love. She woke up and said that love is faith and patience, and if we just have enough faith and patience with each other everything will be okay.

Beth is going to rent an apartment in Wyandotte while I stay in Grand Rapids and get our house ready to put on the market. The apartment she found is tiny, half of a carriage house, two blocks from the river, and I can't get over how strange this is. I *never* would have guessed this. How odd that Beth will be living in my hometown, while I'm living here in hers.

January 18, 2007

Beth has moved to Wyandotte and started her new job. I spent a week with her there and now I am at home alone with plenty of time to work on the search. But I dread making calls to old officers so much that I have given up on it for the time being. What I have decided to do instead is go to Las Vegas in April for the Sabre Pilots Association reunion.

There's a good chance my father could belong to this association, or that someone there might know him. I just can't pass up the opportunity to talk to old pilots and ask if they remember a Greek officer from Nellis, even though the thought of actually talking to them makes me nervous.

February 14, 2007

I have made up a leaflet to hand out at the pilots' reunion in Las Vegas. It features the photo of my mother with Jack Kogan, my cell phone number, and explains that I'm doing research about 1950s Las Vegas. My plan is that I'll hand out copies of this flyer and ask the pilots if they can identify the casino or remember the radio show—all a ploy to get them talking to me. Beth is going to come with me. We're turning it into a vacation. We plan to arrive three days before the pilots' reunion begins so we'll have a chance to relax and see the sights.

February 16, 2007

I've been having a lot of flying dreams lately. In these dreams I realize I have always known how to fly. *It's so easy!* You just have to spread your arms and soar. It feels magnificent, and I'm very good at it. I fly and fly and fly. Sometimes I still have vestiges of belief in my ability after I wake up. I swear I've just got to *lift*. I actually stood in the hall one morning and tried it.

March 10, 2007

It's been a year since I started this project, and I feel like I'm just now starting to make some progress. Last week I finally looked into the identity of the ventriloquist's dummy in the KORK picture. I did a bit of research and decided it looked like Jerry Mahoney, the dummy of Paul Winchell, a well-known 1950s ventriloquist and television personality. I discovered the blog of Paul Winchell's daughter, April, and sent her an e-mail with a copy of the picture. She responded: "Yes, that certainly is a Jerry Mahoney doll. Though it's probably a toy, not the original. I wish I could tell you more. It's a wonderful photo."

CHAPTER 20

Mystère

Las Vegas turned out to be exactly as I expected: architectur-ally extravagant resorts, Disneyesque-themed casinos, wed-ding chapels, Elvis impersonators, and tourists from all over the globe. We saw a lot of construction cranes in the air when we were there in April of 2007, and I noticed a lot of want ads in the local paper. There were plenty of opportunities for work in hotels and casinos, which is how it must have been in the 1950s. I'm sure the chance to make a living in a glamorous town like Las Vegas, a place that drew the top entertainers of the day, would have been appealing to a young woman like my mother. I imagine her as star-struck and captivated by all things American. And I have no doubts about that.

According to Aunt Hilary, my mother had a good time in Las Vegas: "She had quite a full social life. She really enjoyed being there." Unfortunately, the letters my mother wrote to Hilary from Las Vegas have been lost.

My aunt Chris, my mother's other younger sister, said it shocked her to learn that Ann had gotten pregnant in Las Vegas. According to Chris, my mother was the last person you would expect to end up in her situation. "She was the obedient one," Chris said. "Always adhered to the rules. Never got too excited about anything."

Little remains of the Las Vegas my mother knew. Fremont Street, the heart of the action before the development of Las Vegas Boulevard, was closed to vehicle traffic in 1994. Covered over with a nine-story steel canopy, it is promoted to tourists as "The Fremont Street Experience" and features a nightly light-and-sound show. The day we were there, a Grand Prix car race took place nearby, and the streets were crowded with fans.

Thanks to the vintage photos I had obsessively studied, I could visualize Fremont Street as it used to be. Many of the buildings from the 1950s were still standing, but the facades had changed and the interiors had been remodeled. When Beth sat down to play a few hands of blackjack in Binion's, I wandered around looking for traces of how it might have been in 1954, when it was known as the Horseshoe. A wall of dark paneling looked like it might have been there fifty years or more, and the bar might have been original, but otherwise it looked like any other modern casino: a maze of electronically humming slot machines.

While we were in Binion's, Beth and I had a snack at the lunch counter, which also might have been original to the building. Two guys in white paper hats worked behind the counter grilling burgers and hot dogs, looking as if *they* could have been there since the 1950s. I got an order of corn chips drizzled with hot liquid cheese and an icy-cold Coke. My most sinful Las Vegas indulgence.

I could have spent a lot more time exploring Fremont Street, and regret that I didn't, but we were on vacation and there were other things to see and do. We had a nice weekend, and then on Monday everything changed.

According to the schedule of events I printed from the Sabre Pilots Association website, registration for the reunion was set to begin at 1:00 p.m. After breakfast, I headed down to the second floor of our hotel, where the reunion events would take place. When I came upon two long tables and an easel set up outside some meeting rooms, I began to feel as if I were about to go on stage in a play without being sure of my lines. I had never expressed to anyone, not even to Beth, how anxious I felt about my plan to infiltrate this gathering, or how fervently I wished it would lead to success.

Beth suggested we lurk at the hotel registration desk to see if we could spot any old pilots checking in, and sure enough, we did. Most of them wore Sabre Pilot insignia on their hats or shirts. But even without the insignia they were easy to recognize. These were sharp-looking guys for their age, well-dressed, with perfect posture and self-satisfied demeanors.

I sat on an upholstered bench and stared at these men, men who possibly *knew* my father. He could have been standing there among them, smiling and shaking someone's hand, his lovely wife at his side. And as I sat there, spying on old men, it began to seem childish to me, this hunt for a father, this primitive need. I yearned so much for one of these men to be my father that the yearning made me uncomfortable. I felt embarrassed by how *much* I wanted this.

We walked away from the lobby, and we were strolling through the casino when Beth casually asked, "So, what's gonna happen now?"

The question annoyed me. *How could she not know what was going to happen next?* The pilots' registration began at 1:00. I was waiting for that time to begin distributing my leaflets. Wasn't she *with me*? I suggested that maybe we should get a drink and sit by the pool for a little while.

"No," Beth said, "then I'd just wish I was in it."

She said this with a wistful tone, which annoyed me further. It sounded as if being with me in that moment was a sacrifice on her part. And I snapped.

"Well why don't you just go do whatever it is *you* want to do and leave me alone."

Suddenly furious, I waked away from her in tears. I took the elevator up to our room, where my emotions whirled wildly out of control. I felt abandoned. Vulnerable. Desperate.

"How am I supposed to know what the hell is going on when you won't even talk to me about it!" Beth had followed me up to our room. "Every time I ask you what the plan is, you don't want to talk about it. You blow me off."

"Because there is no *plan*!" I yelled. "I deliver the leaflets. I talk to pilots. *That's* it!"

I told Beth to just leave me alone, then felt heartsick as soon as she walked toward the door. I called her back and we both broke down. I was mad at her, mad at me, and mad that this was happening now. *Why now?*

Looking back at that moment in the casino, I realize we were crazy to schedule a crucial, nerve-racking event into the middle of a vacation. Beth had simply been hinting for a little more gambling time, unaware of my fragile psychological state. From her perspective, I had just inexplicably flipped out.

Beth and I needed to hug and patch things up, but the clock was ticking and my face was a mess. I had spent hours before the trip planning exactly what I would wear for this moment. I had purchased new slacks and sandals so I would feel as confident as possible approaching the pilots. Now I was a wreck. I held a damp washcloth against my puffy eyes, took several deep breaths, kissed my bewildered partner, and got on the elevator to the second floor.

The Sabre Pilots registration table was now loaded with information packets, name tags, memorabilia, and insignia items for sale. Behind it were two people —a woman who eyed me suspiciously and a friendly looking man. I wanted to be able to place a stack of my leaflets on the registration table, and I worried about not being allowed to do this. I worried I would be pegged as an interloper. A spy. A bastard child come to pin the blame on one of the fraternity.

I introduced myself to the friendly man, told him I was doing research for a book about Las Vegas in the 1950s, and asked if I could place some leaflets on the table. "Oh, I'm sure that'd be just fine," he said. "You can leave them right here and I'll point them out to the fellas as they come by."

I had worried for nothing. "Thanks," I said. I put the leaflets on the table and wondered if I would have enough. I asked the man how many were expected to attend the reunion.

"About five hundred," he said, "but that's including the wives."

"Whatcha' got there?" one of the registering pilots asked me.

I picked up a leaflet and handed it to him. "I'm writing a book about Las Vegas and I'm trying to identify the casino in this picture, or see if anyone remembers this radio show."

"Oh, I never listened to the radio much." He handed the leaflet back to me, his eyes sparkling and flirtatious.

"Were you here in 1954?" I asked.

"Nope, nope, I was here in '56. I'm one of the youngsters. I'm only seventy-two!"

"Well, I'd love to hear your recollections." I handed the paper back to him, pointed out my cell phone number, and told him I'd be at the hotel until Thursday.

I'm sure this man would have been willing to talk to me further. I probably could have stood right there and talked to lots of men as they registered, but I felt too uneasy about it.

"I'll check back later and see how it's going," I told the man behind the table.

I left the registration area to linger in the second-floor lobby near the elevators. All the pilots passed through this lobby on their way to or from the registration table. I felt less like an intruder there and got up the nerve to actually speak to several pilots, but I heard the same story over and over: they didn't remember the radio show, had no idea about the picture, and didn't recall any Greek officers. I had to repeat my spiel a little louder for one of the guys, and his wife said, "I call them the 'Huh Club,' because none of 'em can hear anymore!"

Approaching pilots turned out to be easier than I expected, and I regretted getting so worked up about it. We had tickets to a Cirque du Soleil show that night and tried to get back into happy-vacation mode, though things were never quite the same. Beth and I were emotionally spent by the day's events but enjoyed the performance of *Mystère*—which, ironically, featured the character of an infant seeking a parent.

As the audience applauded at the end of the show, I felt my cell phone vibrating in my pocket. By the time I got to it, the caller had left a message. "This is Mr. Ed Morrah. I'm here with the Sabre Pilots' reunion. I was here in the fifties, and I don't know if I have anything to add, but I'd be glad to chat with you and see if there's anything I can do to help."

I called Mr. Morrah the next morning and set up a time to meet with him later in the afternoon. Beth and I took it easy that day, never leaving the hotel, and I ran into Sabre pilots everywhere. I discovered the best way to engage them in conversation was by asking how Las Vegas had changed since the 1950s. "In those days it was all about gambling and sex. Not someplace you'd bring your kids," one guy told me.

"On weekends, the people in the casinos would be in tuxedos and full-length gowns."

"I sat and listened to Nat King Cole for more than an hour once just for the cost of a fifty-cent drink." The entertainers stood out most prominently in the pilots' memories of Vegas. They all claimed to have seen Sinatra, as well as Mae West, Milton Berle, and Rosemary Clooney.

I gained confidence in talking to pilots, though none remembered the radio show or a big Greek. A list of those attending the reunion had been posted near the registration table, and none of them sounded familiar to me. None appeared to be Greek. I'd been hoping I might get a look at Demetrios, but no such luck.

Ed Morrah had straight sandy hair, a Carolina accent, and a kind, unassuming manner. He was seventy-five but didn't look it. You'd probably guess him at somewhere in his sixties. We exchanged pleasantries when we met and then sat down at a bar to talk. He said he didn't recognize the casino in the picture or remember the radio show, but he'd be glad to tell me what he could about that time.

He had arrived in Las Vegas in the middle of December 1954. "The first day I got to town they were making a movie on Fremont Street—*The Girl Rush* with Rosalind Russell—and I just thought, *wow...*"

He was twenty-two and learning to fly a fighter jet solo. He described his first flight as exciting: "The plane had a real good feel to it." But the most important thing to Ed was the satisfaction of having accomplished the next step. "The training program was a personal challenge for me," he said. "I wanted to see if I could compete with the best of my contemporaries and become one of the best of the best."

Ed told me stories about practice flights. "We were told to just fly around and see what we could do. Fly up as high as we could." He told one story about approaching a train and pulling up at the last moment.

I asked how often he thought back on those flying days and he said, "Often." But he didn't continue to fly in civilian life. "After high-performance aircraft, what do you do for kicks?"

Ed and I were hitting it off, so I told him I wasn't just writing about the history of Las Vegas, I told him about the search for my father, and when I did, he wished me luck. "It takes courage to do what you're doing," he said. And coming from someone as courageous as him, it meant a lot.

We shook hands and parted ways, though I did see Ed once more during the reunion. While walking down the hall the next day on my way to the pool, I bumped into him. He said he wanted to give me the name of a flight instructor who'd been at Nellis in 1954, and there were some pictures he wanted to show me.

So I went into Ed's room and looked at photos of him as a handsome young pilot with his F-86—nice sharp color shots that looked as if they could have been taken yesterday. "Slide film," Ed explained as I marveled at the quality. I looked at those pictures and immediately fell for the young pilot who was Ed. *Oh, it is so easy*, I thought, *so easy to fall for these guys. These hot-rod flyboys.*

I talked to the flight instructor Ed referred me to later that day. "I understand you're looking for your father," he said, "and I'm sorry I can't help you out."

"You don't remember any Greek men who were here in 1953 or '54?"

"No, ma'am, I don't."

I was beginning to think the trip would be a washout—no luck for me in in Vegas—but then I happened to talk to a pilot named Charles McNeil the next day at the pool. Standing alone near the outdoor bar, he wore a Sabre Pilot cap and looked relaxed, so I introduced myself.

A past president of the Sabre Pilots Association, Charles was glad to talk to me about the old days. He said these guys enjoyed getting together and telling their stories because they remembered them so clearly.

"Do you remember an officer named Demetrios Elipoulos?" I asked.

"No…but I knew a fellow who was here in late '53, a Greek fellow, named William Vasiliatis. He'd come from Harvard. Lives in Virginia now, but he's never been to a reunion."

I had been standing there politely chatting with Charles without taking notes, but I didn't want to forget what he'd just said. "Excuse me a moment." I walked a few feet to the pool bar, where I snagged a pen and something to write on. "What was that name again?"

He spelled it for me: V-a-s-i-l-i-a-t-i-s.

I flew home repeating it over and over in my mind. *Vasiliatis. Vasiliatis.* A mantra of hope.

CHAPTER 21

Professional Help

Soon after I got home from Las Vegas, I found an address and phone number for William Vasiliatis in Arlington, Virginia. I also ran an image search and found a photo of him on an Air Force pilot's site. Standing in the back row of a group shot, William is squinting, so it's hard to tell what he looks like, but I could see that he was tall and had dark hair.

I printed this photo, then turned it upside down on my desk in an attempt to avoid the obsession it could inspire. I tamped down the urge to daydream about success and reunion, knowing how disappointing those daydreams can be. But I couldn't help indulging just a little. I imagined how proud I would be to have a father who went to Harvard, and how well that would reflect upon me.

I wondered why I had missed William's name in the 1954 *Air Force Register* and went to the library to look him up. When I didn't find his name, I wondered if it could be some kind of clerical error. Or did Charles McNeil have a bad memory?

Not finding William in the register took a lot of the air out of my inflated mood, but it didn't discourage me. I had Mr.

Vasiliatis's phone number. I could have just called him, but didn't have the nerve. I felt immobilized for days, and then finally decided to get some professional help. I decided to hire a private investigator, which is what Beth had suggested I do at the beginning of the search.

I opened our *Yellow Pages* directory to the ads for private investigators, called a few, and settled on a young woman, Kate, the owner of Expert Investigations. She made an appointment to meet with me that day at a local coffee shop, where I told her my story.

A medium-sized blonde with a button-down shirt tucked neatly into jeans, Kate had a firm handshake and seemed to be a pretty sharp cookie. In addition to calling William Vasiliatis for me, she suggested some other leads to pursue, including looking into the Las Vegas public records to see if there was anything there about my mother.

I felt relieved to have Kate on the job, but she wasn't free to begin the investigation for two weeks, time during which I couldn't stop myself from woolgathering about William and the Vasiliatis family. Of course I imagined them as intelligent, appealing people with interesting careers and hobbies. I played out long, elaborate scenarios in which this family welcomed me into their lives. I imagined my sons meeting their grandfather for the first time, saw them shaking his hand, talking to him about airplanes. How thrilled they would be.

After more than two weeks went by, I started to get nervous. *What had I done?* I met some chick in a coffee shop and gave her a retainer check without signing a contract or asking for anything that would let me know she was legit. I began to develop a sick feeling about the whole thing. Then, finally, I got an e-mail.

"I have located Mr. Vasiliatis and have been trying to contact him."

Later that day, I got a second e-mail. "I spoke with William, but he was not in Las Vegas in 1954. He was shipped to Europe in May of '53 for a covert operation and didn't return until August of '56. He denies knowing a woman from England, or any woman named Ann Preston while in Las Vegas. He seemed pretty honest and had a good memory."

What is the chemical of disappointment?
I wondered about this as I lay on my bed feeling it, that familiar physical sensation that comes from the chest, which must be why it is known as heartache. This feeling must be caused by a specific chemical that is released with sadness. *But why?* I wondered. *What is the purpose of this?*

After the bad news from Kate, I went to a meeting of an adoption support group known as AIM, the Adoption Identity Movement. This is a Michigan organization, formed in the 1970s. I'd gone to a few AIM meetings in Detroit way back when, and it surprised me to learn it still existed. An eighty-year-old woman named Peg ran the Grand Rapids chapter. She had been leading the group for more than thirty years and worked as a certified confidential intermediary—a court-appointed go-between, allowed access to sealed adoption records. When hired by adoptees or birth parents, Peg would find the sought-after person, make the initial contact, and ask if they wished to be found.

The Grand Rapids AIM group met in the basement of Peg's suburban condo, where framed newspaper stories about her were on display. Peg passed around a sign-in sheet and a donation box at the start of each meeting, but that's as formal as it got. The group was all about talking and listening.

Peg began the meeting by reporting about the recent reunion of a man and his son that she had arranged. Then one of the women in the group talked about not being able to get a passport because of her amended birth certificate—issued a year after her birth. Next, one of the men talked about the emptiness, the missing piece in his life. Around the circle we went. A guy in his forties who had recently met his birth family said, "Within an hour it seemed right. Instant family. Fit right in."

The day after the meeting I called Mike, my ex-husband, and tried to convince him to use Peg to contact his birth parents. I had been bugging him to try and find his parents for years, but he hadn't yet taken any steps in that direction. I suggested he come to an AIM meeting with me, but they were held on his golf night. "Maybe in the fall," he said.

I wrote a letter to Charles McNeil, the pilot I met at the Monte Carlo pool, and it turned out he had his dates wrong. He was off by a year. He wrote back and apologized. He didn't know of any other pilots with Greek names, but wished me luck. Same old story, over and over. Nothing but dead ends. And nothing in the way of results from the detective. A few weeks later I got an e-mail from her: "As far as obtaining a list of officers stationed at Nellis Air Force Base in 1954, we have exhausted all avenues."

No surprise. I felt sorry she had wasted her time—and my dime.

CHAPTER 22

Biological Family

In June of 2007 I received the shocking news that my uncle, Timothy Preston, my grandmother's youngest son, had been killed in an auto accident in Chicago. When Uncle Tim's wife, Linda, called to tell me, I could hardly believe that another Preston sibling had died this way. In addition to Margaret and Ann, their brother Billy died in a 1972 automobile accident, and their brother John was fatally struck while crossing a street in 1989. Tim was the fifth out of eight siblings to be killed as the result of a vehicle accident.

Five out of eight. *What are the odds of that?*

Tim's accident happened in the West Chicago suburbs, in the middle of the afternoon, when a truck with bad brakes sped through a red light and smashed into his van. Tim's twenty-seven-year-old son, who has Down syndrome, was also in the van and survived with only cuts and bruises, though I can't imagine a more horrible experience for him. Tim's life had revolved around caring for his son. At the time of the accident they were on their way to do their daily paper route.

I first heard of Tim Preston from Jane sometime when I was a teenager. She told me about this guy, our *uncle,* who traveled around the country on a motorcycle. Jane said Uncle Tim was expected to visit Michigan soon and might come to meet me—a thrilling possibility. I fantasized about hopping onto a motorcycle with him, my *real* uncle, and impressing everyone in the neighborhood as we went roaring off, my hair flying wild in the wind. But Tim Preston never arrived, and when I did finally meet him, in 1983, he wasn't anything like the cool, handsome James Dean type I had imagined.

With a head full of frizzy hair, bushy eyebrows, an English accent, and a theatrical personality, Tim Preston stood out in a crowd. He wore outdated eyeglasses, rumpled clothing, and a fanny pack he used like a purse.

We met for the first time at Hoffmaster State Park in Muskegon, a place where steep sand dunes rise along the Lake Michigan shore. My sons were two years old at the time, Tim's son was about the same age, and I think Tim had as much fun as the kids, climbing the dunes and then rolling down, again and again.

During the time I knew Tim Preston, he appeared to have a good relationship with his mother. He lived near her in Chicago and saw her often. But I don't think he ever got over the experience of being left behind in England, at the age of fourteen, when my grandmother emigrated. He didn't join her in New York until three years later.

Like my cousin Benny, Tim spent much of his life wandering from place to place, and job to job. I got to know him because he finally settled down nearby. Chicago is just a three-hour drive from west Michigan, but we didn't see each other as often as Tim would have liked, and I'm sorry about that.

About a year before Tim's accident, I wrote a long, newsy letter to him and Linda. Beth and I had just returned from a trip to New York, during which we explored Montague Street in Brooklyn Heights and found my grandmother's old apartment. Linda responded to my letter by e-mail, and at the end of the e-mail was a note from Tim:

> So nice to hear from you! You write such nice letters. Montague Street! It all seems like a dream now, so much has happened since. You still seem to be homesick for the family you never had. I am only just getting over it myself. Love goes a long way towards reconciliation.

After Tim's death, only three Preston siblings remained: Hilary in Florida, David in London, and Chris in Bristol, England. They rarely communicated with one another, and since Linda felt too distraught to call them, it fell to me to let them know about their brother's death.

In addition to my aunt Hilary and my uncle David, I called my cousin Paul in New York to tell him the news. Paul is the son of my aunt Chris, a woman who suffers from bipolar disorder and refuses to have anything to do with me. I have only met Chris once, and that meeting was a disaster.

Like nearly all of her siblings, Chris Preston immigrated to the United States in the 1950s. She settled in Brooklyn, got married, had two children, and eventually divorced. She called me on the phone a few times after I connected with my grandmother in the 1980s, but those calls were mostly one-sided conversations on her part, with lots of plans to visit that never materialized.

Chris eventually moved back to England and settled in Bristol, followed a few years later by her daughter, Liz. In 2001 I made plans to visit Bristol as part of a trip I took to England. I had never journeyed outside the United States (other than Canada) before this trip, and spent several months obsessively preparing for it.

My grandmother would have enjoyed going with me, but had become too frail for travel. I planned to go solo, which I didn't mind at all. I looked forward to being on my own in London, but my grandmother insisted I spend time with my uncle David. She had recently reconnected with him after a long absence in communication. "Lovely man," she said. "Terrific gardener." So I arranged to have Uncle David pick me up at Heathrow.

Too keyed up to sleep on the plane, I arrived in London feeling tremendously jet-lagged as well as nervous about meeting my uncle for the first time. I expected him to be outgoing and expansive, like Tim, but Uncle David had a reserved demeanor. He treated me politely but did not seem especially pleased with my visit. He drove me to his tiny house in the South London suburb of Beddington, where I tried to sleep but didn't get much, and suffered from an allergic reaction to his cat.

I went out to dinner with Uncle David and his wife, Phyllis, that evening, but it's all a bit foggy, what with the jet lag and the antihistamines. The next morning, after Uncle David went off to his job, I suggested to Phyllis that perhaps it would be best if I got a hotel room, and she didn't object.

I happily spent the next two days exploring London on my own. I stayed in a little hotel next to Charing Cross Station, and fell in love with the city. I saw a play, went to three museums, hung out in Trafalgar Square, and took lots of pictures.

On my third day in London I took a train to Bristol, where Aunt Chris's daughter, Liz, met me at the station. Liz has dark hair from her Italian father, with Mary Preston's blue eyes and a small, seemingly fragile frame.

We took a cab to the charming flat she shared with her boyfriend, who was away on business during my visit. Liz showed me around, and then we went out to dinner at an Indian restaurant where we talked about our disjointed family, our complicated lives, and the things we had in common. Our conversation flowed easily, and I felt thrilled to have discovered a cousin, just a few years younger than me, whose company I enjoyed so much.

Aunt Chris arrived the next morning, as trim and attractive as her photographs had depicted. But our meeting did not go as warmly as I had hoped. Chris seemed anxious, unable to sit still or even stand in one place for long, and she regarded me with a cool, judgmental eye, similar to the response I had gotten from my uncle David.

I didn't understand this response, and *still* don't understand it. Could the icy reception I received have something to do with my relationship with my grandmother? Did it seem odd to David and Chris, both of whom had troubled relationships with their mother, that she had formed a close bond with me?

Chris had planned the day. She would drive us to the city of Bath, where we would take a tour on a bus—a very specific bus. It couldn't be just any tour bus, it had to be the one Chris had particularly enjoyed the last time she'd been there, a double-decker bus with recorded narration. She made quite a point about it and described it in detail.

Chris drove us to Bath in her car. We took the tour bus, saw the ancient Roman baths, and everything went well. We were having a nice day. We were sitting at a café table in front of a beautiful Georgian hotel when Liz suggested I go to the bar and order a Pimm's cocktail, which I did. I brought the drink back to the table, delighted with its fruity effervescence. I sipped at it while I listened to Aunt Chris tell us about other places where there were hot springs in England.

When Chris finished talking, I turned to Liz and asked her about the Pimm's. "What's in this? It's great!" I said. And suddenly, Aunt Chris smacked her hands down on the table, turning her head away from us.

"What's wrong?" Liz asked.

"I'm annoyed."

"What's annoying you?"

Chris turned her head back with a scowl. "She's not listening to me. She's not paying attention to what I say!"

"Oh, Mother…"

"What's she talking to you for?" Chris shouted. "I'm her aunt. And she just ignores me. Like I don't exist!"

I tried to apologize, to say it wasn't so, but it made no difference. Her anger increased, and people at adjoining tables began to stare. In spite of my attempts to be reasonable and conciliatory, Chris would not calm down. She pointed her finger at me and said, "Your mother was a sweet, kind person, and you're nothing like her."

Devastated by this, I could not speak. Liz and Chris continued to shout as I got up from the table and walked away in a daze. It had all gone wrong so quickly.

Liz and Chris followed after me, still yelling at one another. We were standing on the sidewalk beside the café when Chris began hitting Liz. And it seemed so absurd. There we were in the middle of that lovely city, on a lovely spring afternoon, and Chris was smacking her daughter on the head. The last I saw of my aunt, she was charging across the street in a fury. She disappeared down an alley and left us standing there, stunned. And stranded.

The experience traumatized me, but Liz wasn't as upset as you'd expect, apparently accustomed to this kind of behavior from her mother. We went inside the hotel, sat at the bar, and had a few drinks while we talked it over.

"She does this kind of thing all the time," Liz said. "She's terribly insecure and has been really nervous about meeting you."

We considered the possibility that it might have been overwhelming for Chris to be reminded of her long-dead sister, or that I had disappointed her by *not* being like Ann. In any case, her behavior hurt me deeply. And my immediate reaction was to take the blame. Deep down, I know I am a terrible person: selfish and badly behaved.

Liz and I had to find a bus to take us back to Bristol—a long, depressing ride. When we finally arrived at her flat, Liz found an urgent telephone message from her brother, Paul. It turned out that Paul, who lived in Manhattan, just happened to be in London with his girlfriend that day, but felt unsure about visiting his mother since she was now in a state of agitation. I don't know if Paul had come to England knowing I would be there, or if his visit was coincidental, but he didn't make any effort to meet me or talk to me.

Liz rented a car the next day, and we drove to Stratford-upon-Avon, as had been our plan, only Chris didn't join us. Even though Chris had reserved a room in Stratford, she refused to come along. Liz and I spent two days there, seeing the sights and having a good time in spite of the disturbing scene in Bath. We toured the theaters, visited Shakespeare's grave, and saw a production of Hamlet we both enjoyed—*a family even more dysfunctional than ours!*

At the end of our stay in Stratford, I took the train back to London, where it was rainy and gloomy and I sunk into a blue mood. I had booked myself into an upscale hotel on Southampton Row for the last few days of my trip, looking forward to exploring the Bloomsbury neighborhood. I had imagined myself sitting in parks and soaking up the atmosphere. Instead, I walked around under an umbrella feeling lonely. I went to the British Museum and St. Paul's Cathedral, but at the end of each day there was just me and my pitiful self. I got sad little takeaway meals and ate them in my room.

When my grandmother died in June of 2004, I had lost touch with Liz and didn't know how to contact Aunt Chris. So I looked up Paul's number in Manhattan and called him. He answered the phone, and I identified myself. I told him that Grandma had died and asked him to please let his mother and Liz know. He thanked me for calling, gave me Liz's current e-mail address, and ended the conversation. We exchanged information politely, but it seemed odd not to say a single personal word.

I e-mailed Liz and got this reply:

Good to hear from you despite the sad news about Grandma. I just called my mother and told her. I must apologize for not staying in touch, but things have been in a bit of turmoil. Regarding Grandma, it's sad that the family isn't closer and never has been. Everyone has their own family issues and I'm not surprised that no one was there for Grandma at the end. I'm sad that I didn't get to see her again before she had that stroke, but what's done is done. So, what has happened to all her things? Photographs and such.

Liz sent this e-mail from an office where she worked as a receptionist, the only contact address I had for her. A few months later she was no longer there.

In the fall of 2005, Beth and I took a weeklong trip to New York City. We stayed in a hotel near the address I had for Paul, and I thought about calling him to say hello, but feared being rejected. I picked up the phone a few times to dial, then chickened out. It wasn't until our last full day in the city that I decided to at least walk by his apartment to see if he still lived there. I found his building, went into the lobby, located his name on a mailbox, stood there a moment, then turned around and walked back to the hotel.

"That's crazy," Beth said. She insisted that I call him, and when I did, he seemed pleased to hear from me.

"Hilary? Hi!"

Paul told me that Liz just happened to be in town visiting him. She had been in town the whole week I'd been there. He put her on the phone, we made plans to meet for drinks, and within an hour I found myself sitting in a bar on Fifty-Fourth Street with my cousins and Beth.

Paul turned out to be low key, but not unfriendly. Handsome, with the same dark hair and blue eyes as Liz, he worked in finance. Paul and Liz were on their way to Brooklyn that evening to have dinner with their father, and I envied them that. I didn't know anything about their father or their life with him, but at least they had a father, and their father's family, not just the disconnected Prestons.

Liz met us for breakfast the next morning, and then we spent a few hours in Central Park before Beth and I had to go to the airport. We sat near the statue of Alice in Wonderland and caught up. Liz was getting ready to take off on a trip to Romania. She planned to work as a volunteer at a Romanian orphanage, and she also talked of going to South America sometime soon. We talked about books and plays—ordinary things. It was a seemingly ordinary moment: a conversation between cousins. But for me it exemplified the kind of life I had been missing for so long.

I think the Preston family dynamic would have been much better if my mother and Margaret hadn't died. I'm sure it would have been less fractured, and I wonder what that would have been like. Would we have been one big happy family? I assume my mother would have eventually gotten married, and I wonder how *that* would have turned out. There are so many possible scenarios. Things might have gone badly for her. Or for me. Or things might have been okay; I might have done well in school and attended some state university.

Benny once told me a story about his dad receiving divorce papers in the mail after Margaret died. He said he heard this story from his dad, but it seems unlikely that divorce papers would arrive unexpectedly this way.

I don't doubt that there were troubles between Jim and Margaret, though. I'm sure she yearned for a more glamorous life than she got from a guy in grease-stained clothes. And I can't imagine her leaving California to settle down with Jim in Michigan.

In one of the old photo albums, I found a postcard my grandmother wrote in September of 1954 (two months before my birth.) On the front of this postcard is a photo of my grandmother and Hilary standing outside a building somewhere in London. For some reason, they are wearing baggy blue jeans with the legs rolled up—a highly unusual look for them.

On the back of this card, my grandmother wrote:

Dear Margaret,

What do you think of this snap? Your house sounds delightful. I expect to join you with Timothy next year. Hilary says she wants to look at Europe before leaving it, so she will come later. We are waiting to hear what Chris' plans are. Timmy is back at a good school and will be in the Xmas play. Tell Ann to write.

All my love,
Mother

My grandmother told me she had been planning to settle in San Francisco, and I imagine that Hilary, Tim, and Chris would have all ended up there as well. And I can't help thinking of all those lives, the trajectory of all those lives, altered by one accident.

Search Journal: October 12, 2007

I would rather do just about anything than call strangers and ask strange questions. Cleaning out closets is much more appealing. As is yard work, stripping wallpaper, and painting woodwork. But every once in a while, when I force myself to sit down and make a few calls, there is something intriguing. Like the conversation I recently had with a woman who confirmed her deceased husband was Greek and had been at Nellis in 1954. I didn't know what to ask next. *Did he fool around? Ever mention an English girl?* I sent her a follow-up letter along with pictures of me, Justin, and Jeremy.

While making these calls the other day, I finally found the nerve to contact Mary Valverde – the woman who lived in Sunnyvale and offered to adopt me after the accident. Unfortunately, she is ninety years old now and couldn't recall anything I asked about. She didn't remember my mother, didn't remember Margaret, and when I asked about the accident, she said, "I don't remember that at all. Isn't that awful?" I sadly crossed her off my list.

I have also recently made a few calls to men named John Wales, the name of the sailor who was driving the car the night of the accident. There are more than a hundred men with this name in the United States. I have called about ten of them so far with no luck, and I'm wondering if it's worth the effort. I doubt that Mr. Wales knew anything about my father, and I dread the idea of dredging up what must be a horrible memory for him.

November 18, 2007

Mike finally went to an AIM meeting with me. I think I have convinced him to engage a confidential intermediary to search for his birth parents, but I'm not sure. He talks as if this is something he wants to do but then doesn't follow through. At the AIM meeting, he talked about never feeling like he fit in with his family, and his fear of being rejected by his birth parents.

After the meeting, Mike called the court in Kalamazoo to ask about getting an intermediary, and they sent him a packet of forms. The last time I met him for lunch, we went over the forms together and he filled them out. All he has to do now is put the forms in the mail with a three-hundred dollar check, but he hasn't taken that step yet.

Mike and I usually meet at Panera Bread near the mall in Kalamazoo. We sit in a booth and talk about our lives, our sons, and things that happened in the past. "Remember that time we went to a marriage counselor and the guy thought we were crazy?" he asked me recently. I have no memory of this but found it amusing, as if I were listening to someone else's funny story.

January 12, 2008

The terms "mortgage crisis" and "housing slump" are being used frequently in the news these days. Our house has been on the market since June, but we haven't had any offers. Beth has been coming home from Wyandotte most weekends, or sometimes I go there, though there is hardly room for both of us in her tiny apartment.

We have been living in separate places for a year now, and I've had the best part of the deal, puttering around in our four-bedroom house, while Beth has been cooped up in her rented rooms. Beth has had the stress of a new job, in a new place, while I have had the advantage of writing in isolation. We have jokingly referred to the house as my "Vermont," as if I've been living in a remote artist's retreat.

For me it's been ideal, solitude and partnership simultaneously fulfilled. In spite of the fact that I thrive best with a lot of time to myself, I have never been happy without a significant other, and Beth is unquestionably the most significant. She is smart, friendly, funny, generous, forgiving, and flexible. Beth is always willing to change her mind. She doesn't sulk. Doesn't hold grudges. Can't keep a secret. Thinks the best of everyone. And can't wait until tomorrow.

We are stronger for having weathered these last two difficult years, one of unemployment, and one of living separately. But we will both be glad to put this time behind us, to live in one place, and build our lives together again.

January 24, 2008

I have gotten replies to some of the follow-up letters I've been sending, and I always have a little moment of fear when I read the subject line or return address. I'm afraid the message will be from someone who is insulted or annoyed. But, on the contrary, the messages have all been kind. Here's an example:

Dear Ms. Harper,

I commend your efforts to find your father, but I can assure you that my father is not the one you're looking for. One, he is not Greek. Also, my parents were stationed in Virginia in 1954. And one last thing, we all have a very strong chin with a dent in it (like Cary Grant) not one of us escapes it. Your boys are much too handsome to be one of us. I truly wish you all the luck in attempting to find your father. I can only imagine the difficulty.

February 15, 2008

We have found a renter for our house, so I've got to get used to the idea that I'm moving back to the east side of the state, possibly to Wyandotte. It's a strange turn of events I never would have predicted, and I'm not sure how I feel about it. The Downriver area has become so much shabbier than I remember it—a gritty relic of the prosperous blue-collar culture of my childhood. It's sad, and yet it inspires me. It inspires my photography, which I've been doing a lot of lately. I like taking abstract photos of rust and decay. I am happiest these days when I am in a junkyard, or walking along the railroad tracks shooting photos of boxcars covered with graffiti. One good thing about living in Metro Detroit again is the abundance of photographic opportunities.

March 12, 2008

I called Mike last week to tell him about the move and invited him to meet me for lunch in Grand Rapids. A few days later we sat at a booth catching up with each other. An hour quickly slipped by with no mention about the confidential intermediary, and then I handed Mike an envelope.

"What's this?" he asked.

"I know it's a little early, but happy birthday."

I hadn't given Mike a birthday card in a while, and he seemed touched by the gesture. But when he opened it and read the message I had written inside—all about how I wished him the courage to open the door of his past—his expression changed.

"Thanks," he said and put the card back in the envelope.

"So? What do you think?"

He took a deep breath, exhaled, and finally said, "I just don't want to do it."

Disappointed, I said nothing.

"I just can't risk the rejection," he said, and then sat quietly for a moment. "I just can't help wondering how come they never looked for me."

I sighed. Mike has said this to me several times, and I don't know why he dwells on it. I repeated what I told him previously: "Your mother has probably wondered about you all these years, but she might not have told her husband and other children about you. When unmarried girls had babies back then it was very hush-hush. I don't think it's unusual that she never looked for you. She had legally relinquished her rights to you. And anyway, how do you know she hasn't looked? Maybe she tried to find you and couldn't do it."

"I guess I'll never know," he said.

"I guess you won't."

I couldn't help feeling frustrated. As someone who has wished so much to be known, I had a hard time understanding Mike's decision to remain unknown.

"It's just easier for me to speculate," he said. "Maybe they *wouldn't* reject me, and that possibility gets me by."

June 12, 2008

When I began this search, I assumed it would end in one of two ways: either I would find my father or I wouldn't. But I realize now that it isn't necessarily an either/or situation. The story can end with a maybe—with the possibility that anything *could* happen.

Maybe Aunt Hilary will finally decide to move into a senior citizens' apartment, and I will go down there to help sort through the things in her trailer. We will be dividing her possessions into piles—things to keep, things to throw away, things to donate—when I'll come across a box of old books. I will pull out a dusty copy of *Doctor Zhivago*, open it up, and see that it's a first edition. "Oh my gosh," I'll say. "Some of these books might be valuable."

"Oh. I forgot I had those," Aunt Hilary will say. She will tell me that Jim Rutledge gave her this box of books. She will say they were Margaret's.

The kettle will whistle and Hilary will go into the kitchen to make tea as I sit with the box, lifting books out and touching them gently. The dust jackets will be worn but intact. I will look at the cover of *My Cousin Rachel* by Daphne du Maurier, and *From Here to Eternity* by James Jones. I will open them up, look to see if anything is inscribed inside, maybe flip through a few pages. And then, from inside one of the books, a letter will fall. It will fall into my lap. Addressed to Mrs. Margaret Rutledge in Hawaii, it will be postmarked from Las Vegas, Nevada.

Or maybe this: Maybe Danielle Grise really *is* my cousin. Maybe she suspects that her uncle—let's call him Demetri—is my father, but she doesn't want to say anything about it. *Why rock the boat?* And then, two years from now, her uncle dies and she finds out at his funeral that he had a secret family. Uncle Demetri's secret bastard children show up at his burial and Danielle is so shocked that she blurts out, "He's got a daughter in Michigan, too!"

Or maybe it's all just wishful thinking—evidence that I haven't really given up. And it's true, I am still wishful. But at least I can rest now, knowing I did everything I could. Of course I'm disappointed that I didn't find my father, but I'm glad to put the emotions of searching behind me. Especially the elation that came when I thought I had found him, and the grief when I knew I had not.

I recently saw a television show about "donor-conceived adults," children born of sperm donation—an estimated million people who have come of age and are asking, "Who am I?" They spoke of grief, loss, longing, and a sense of void in their lives. One young woman said that knowing her father would give her a sense of belonging. Another said, "It would fit the pieces of my life together." And another said, "It should be my right to know who he is."

I am strongly opposed to anonymous sperm or egg donation. I believe it is morally wrong to deny a person half their identity, even though I will most likely never know the paternal half of mine, and have come to accept that as best I can.

CHAPTER 23

Almost Home

I wrote what I thought would be the epilogue to this memoir in July of 2011. Beth and I had settled into our new house in the northern Detroit suburbs, and our lives were busy and full. Beth learned to sail on the Detroit River, volunteered as a tutor for inner-city girls, and rolled with the absurdities of corporate life. I worked as an extra in a couple of movies, went out on urban explorations with a local photography group, and began a graduate degree program in creative writing.

We discovered we enjoyed living in Metro Detroit, and we especially enjoyed becoming grandmas together. In the summer of 2011, our grandson Ben had just turned three, and our granddaughter Natalie was one. Ben's full name is Benjamin Preston Reilly. It delighted me to learn this name on the day he was born. His father, Justin, picked it out, a nice way to pass on the only genuine surname he knew at that time.

Google Street View was a brand-new thing that summer, and I used it to locate the house on Borregas Avenue in Sunnyvale. I zoomed in. The front yard now had a fence and contained some overgrown rosebushes, but other than that it didn't look much different from the place where I stood in 1976, asking that uneasy kid to let me in.

I also zoomed in to the intersection of Bayshore Highway and Lawrence Road—where the accident happened. Bayshore is now U.S. Route 101, and Lawrence Road is now the Lawrence Expressway.

The junction where the two roads meet is a figure eight of exit and entrance ramps. The eight looks like an infinity symbol from above, making it easy to spot. At that location, Margaret and Ann were less than three miles from home.

Part Two

"…our fate is to face the world as orphans, chasing
through long years the shadows of vanished parents.
There is nothing for it but to try and see through
our missions to the end, as best we can, for until
we do so, we will be permitted no calm."

-Kazuo Ishiguro
When We Were Orphans

CHAPTER 24

DNA Results

I became Facebook friends with Danielle Grise in 2012 and sent her this message: "... I can see by your FB pics that we don't look as similar as we once did, though I do still wonder if we're some kind of second cousins or something. What was your mother's maiden name?"

In her reply, Danielle told me her mother's maiden name was Belocas, but she didn't know much about that side of her family, the Greek side. I asked Danielle some questions about her Belocas uncles and did some Internet searches about them, but didn't come up with much. More than a year went by before I became interested in exploring my connection to Danielle again.

In January of 2014 I realized, by way of her Facebook status, that Danielle was in a relationship with a woman. "I'm assuming Donna is your partner?" I wrote. "And if so, isn't that a coincidence! I swear we must be related somehow."

More than five years had gone by since I stopped searching for my father. But here was a loose thread, and I just had to tug on it. I learned that Danielle's grandfather had been an officer in the Navy, and I began to wonder if he could be my father.

This intriguing possibility led me to become preoccupied with Danielle's family, scrutinizing their photos on Facebook. In order to learn as much about them as I could, I joined Ancestry.com and began constructing a Belocas family tree.

That February, I read an article in the *Detroit Free Press* about how recent advances in DNA testing had made it possible for adoptees to discover their biological lineage. These tests not only determine a person's ancestral ethnicity, but also link them with others who share their DNA. The article profiled three companies that were doing this kind of testing, including Ancestry.com.

I ordered a test for myself immediately and asked Danielle to get one as well. I worried that she might not want to do this, considering it could reveal her grandfather to be an adulterer, but she wrote in a Facebook message, "Sound good to me. I'm curious about our connection, too."

My DNA results came in April and revealed a surprise: I am *not* Greek.

According to Ancestry.com, I am 100 percent European, mostly Irish and English—a shocking revelation, since this would mean my search for a Greek father had been pointless.

An enormous waste of time.

This news about my ethnicity was disconcerting. But my DNA matches in the Ancestry database were fascinating. My matches included several close cousins whose family trees did not contain the surnames of any of my maternal ancestors, which meant they had to be my paternal relatives.

Paternal relatives!

I spent a lot of time on the Ancestry site that April and began communicating with my closest match, a woman named Laura Harper. How funny it would be, I thought, if my last name turned out to actually *be* Harper. But Laura quickly nixed that idea. Laura's mother had also been tested by Ancestry and I did not match her, so I had to be related to Laura on her father's side. Since I also did not match with her Harper cousins in the Ancestry database, Laura concluded I had to be related to her paternal grandmother, Dorothy Hadley.

But I didn't understand how this was possible. In an e-mail to Laura, I wrote, "If we are second cousins, that means our parents had to be first cousins, which means our grandparents had to be siblings, and Dorothy Hadley was an only child!"

I hadn't yet begun to learn about the complicated ways in which cousins can be connected. I didn't know what it meant to be a second cousin once removed or a first cousin twice removed, but I was about to find out.

Laura Harper convinced me that we shared the same great-great-grandfather, John Marshall Hadley. This was confirmed when I began communicating with one of my third-cousin matches, Pam Farrow, also a descendent of John Marshall Hadley. Pam and Laura would prove invaluable resources in my search. I am indebted to them both.

In early May, Danielle got her DNA results, which revealed we are not related at all. Not even distantly. As it turns out, we are just random doppelgangers, which disappointed us both. "But we still have a cool story to tell," Danielle wrote to me.

To confirm the ethnicity results I received from Ancestry, I did another DNA test, this time with a genetic-testing service called 23andMe, and the outcome was the same: 100 percent European, predominantly Irish and English, and no Greek.

This corroborating evidence brought certainty. And dismay. I had believed myself to be Greek for thirty years, and I had constructed an image of my Greek father during those years. I *saw* him as that "big Greek" described by Jim Rutledge.

Jim must have been misinformed about my father being Greek. Or maybe my mother did, indeed, have a relationship with a Greek man, but also slept with my father in the month she got pregnant. Maybe that's why his name was scratched off the hospital record in San Jose, and also why there is no "name of father" in my baby book. Ann probably wasn't certain who had fathered her child, which must have been an awkward situation for her. To say the least.

In any case, I felt deep regret about all the time and effort I put into searching for a Greek father who didn't exist. Was the story I told about the search for that father now no longer valid? Or was my earnest belief in false clues an important part of the story? It had been easy to believe any little thing, to latch on to any shred of knowledge, in place of the disquieting void of nothing at all.

CHAPTER 25

Mystery Man

My paternal ancestor, John Marshall Hadley, had seven children, each of whom had multiple offspring, who also produced multiple offspring. Unfortunately, the names of these offspring were not all available on Ancestry.com. The site is designed to dig back into a family tree. It is much more difficult to dig forward. I needed to identify all of John Marshall's male descendants born between 1915 and 1930—the time period in which my father had likely been born. This proved to be a challenging, time-consuming task.

In addition to my online research, I also made family-tree charts on large sheets of drawing paper which were spread out on our dining room table for weeks. I worked on these charts for many hours and found my way to multiple dead ends, but then, in June, I discovered three of my DNA cousin matches were related to a woman named Margaret Rowe.

Margaret Rowe, known as Maggie, was the wife of John Marshall Hadley's son, Charles. My kinship to both Maggie Rowe and Charles Hadley meant my father had to be one of their descendants, most likely one of their grandsons. This discovery significantly narrowed my search parameters. I drew a new chart with Charles and Maggie at the top, followed by a list of their children, and began finding out as much as I could about them.

By late June, I had honed my list down to seven grandsons of Charles and Maggie, all of whom were the right age to be my father. I then faced the challenge of finding contact information for these men and their closest relatives. In order to accomplish this task I signed up with a site that provides this information for a fee and filled several legal pads with notes. It turned out that all of my long lost Hadley relatives lived in either Kansas or California, mostly Southern California. I called a few of these relatives, cousins of one sort or another, and had some interesting conversations, but none that led to conclusive results.

Beth and I usually travel somewhere for the Fourth of July, but in 2014 we were at home. Beth went out to do some yard work while I stayed in and worked on the search. I logged on to Ancestry to see what new information I might be able to gather, focusing my attention on one of Charles and Maggie's grandsons, Fred Hadley.

I had recently come across a photo of Fred on the Ancestry site. In this black-and-white photo, he and his father, Ted Hadley, are sitting in lawn chairs, each with a drink in his hand. The person who posted this photo onto Ancestry went by the username "Catarand." He had labeled the photo "Dad and Ted, Las Vegas 1955," which piqued my interest. I sent a message to Catarand, but had not yet received a reply.

Investigating Ted Hadley on Ancestry, I learned he had lived in Las Vegas. His son Fred, who lived in Kansas, must have been visiting him when the photo was taken. Something about Fred seemed familiar to me. When I enlarged the grainy photograph to study his face, I realized he reminded me of a man in a picture I had found in one of the old photo albums—a photo that had always been a mystery to me.

In the mystery photo, taken in March of 1955, a man sits next to my mother on the sofa in the house in Sunnyvale. Wearing a nice-looking suit and tie, the man has his head turned to the side and is gazing adoringly at her.

Ann is wearing a satin dress that exposes her shoulders, a glittery necklace, and earrings. Her eyes focus on the camera, most likely held by Margaret. The expression on her face conveys a kind of uncomfortable happiness. It looks as if she is so flattered by this man's attention that it's a bit embarrassing for her.

I found it odd that my mother apparently went out on a date with this man just four months after giving birth to me. I always wondered how that would have come about. How would she have met this guy, and why would he be so pleased to be dating the mother of an illegitimate infant? They are sitting close, shoulder to shoulder. He is holding her hand. And there is that gaze. It does not seem to be the gaze of a man looking at a woman he just met.

When I realized that Fred reminded me of the man in the mystery photo, I immediately went to get it. I removed the snapshot from the plastic pocket in the album where I keep it, and compared it to the one of Fred on my laptop. I could definitely see a resemblance, and felt a little flutter in my heart.

I went outside, where Beth was mowing the lawn. I signaled to her from the porch, waving my arms and shouting her name. She shut off the mower and asked what I wanted. I waved her into the house.

"Is this guy, this guy?" I asked, pointing to the two photos. I expected Beth to be skeptical, perhaps annoyed that I had called her in for such a minor thing, but she saw the resemblance, too.

I ticked off the pertinent facts about Fred on my fingers. "He is somehow related to me by DNA. He had reason to be in Las Vegas in the 1950s. And he looks like a man in a photo with my mother."

"I think you're right," Beth said. "He could be the one."

I Googled Fred Hadley and couldn't believe what I found. Beth had just returned to the yard when I ran out on the porch and yelled, "He's got a blog!"

Fred Hadley's blog, titled the *Life and Times of Fred Hadley*, is actually several blogs, one for each decade of his life. They read like an autobiography and include transcripts of his diaries, with many photographs. I had no problem gathering information about him. Born in Wichita in 1922, Fred served in the Navy, got a degree in electrical engineering, worked for Boeing until he retired, had *six* wives, two sons, and many affairs, about which he boasted proudly. He filled his diaries with details about all the many women he bedded.

I spent most of the day reading about him, feeling both fascinated and repelled. His 1950s blog mentioned that he made "some trips to Vegas to see Dad," but gave no details about those trips. I wondered, was this lack of detail significant? Had he purposely left out some incriminating information about one of those trips?

I looked up Fred's address and phone number, and Beth convinced me to call him that day. I worked up some courage, sat at my desk, called his number, and was not surprised when a female voice answered. I knew from Fred's blog that he lived with a female companion just seven years older than me. She answered, sounding gravel-voiced and annoyed. I asked to speak to Fred and she said, "He's sleeping."

I apologized, said I could call later, but she said no, no, that wouldn't be necessary. "He likes to get his telephone calls. Hold on." She disappeared, and I heard nothing for what seemed an eternity. Then an elderly male voice said hello with a questioning tone.

My heart fluttered again at the sound of his voice, which could be the voice of my father. *The voice of my father!* I introduced myself and explained that I had been doing some genealogy about the Hadley family in Wichita. "Oh," he said brightly, "are you a Wichitan?" He spoke in a slightly higher register than usual for a man, and with a Kansas accent. When I told him I was calling from Michigan, he seemed disappointed. And somewhat confused.

I explained about finding Hadley relatives on Ancestry.com, and he said, "Oh, yeah. My son has done some of that." I told him I wanted to determine where I fit in the Hadley family tree. "Okay," he said, "how can I help you?"

I asked a few innocuous questions first, and then asked if he had been in Las Vegas in 1954. "I coulda' spent a couple of days there," he said. He explained that his father had been a chef in Las Vegas for many years.

"Do you remember a woman named Ann Preston?" I asked.

"Doesn't ring a bell," he replied flatly.

I explained that she was an English girl, which I hoped might jar his ninety-one-year-old memory, but it didn't help. He began to sound suspicious and asked, "What's your occupation?" I told him I was writing a book about the search for my father, and that I had read his blog and found it interesting. "Oh yes," he said, "I've lived an interesting life."

We chatted a bit more after that, and he asked if I would be seeing any fireworks that day. I told him yes, I did plan on that for later, and this seemed to please him. I asked for his e-mail address, thanked him for his time, and wished him a happy Fourth of July.

I ended the call and sat there flabbergasted. *Did I just talk to my father?*

I composed an e-mail to Fred and sent it that day. The next day, I mailed him a letter. In both messages I said I hoped he might be able to help me find my father. "He would most likely be someone from your generation of the Hadley family, so I am wondering if he might have been one of your cousins. Or possibly you?" I told Fred more about my mother, more about myself, and asked some questions about his life. I also sent him some photos of myself, my sons, my mother, and a copy of the photo of the mystery man.

I wondered if Fred had simply forgotten my mother. Considering his age, his memory could certainly be faulty. But Fred kept written records of everything. He had kept diaries all his life, which made Beth laugh when I mentioned this, since this reminded her so much of me.

We went on a week-long trip to the Lake Michigan shore the next day, and I tried to think of things other than having maybe found my father, but it wasn't easy. I showed the photo of Fred and the snapshot of the mystery man to the friends we were visiting, but they did *not* see the resemblance. Differences between the men in the two photos were pointed out to me, which I found hard to accept. If Fred was, indeed, my father, I wanted him to be the man in the mystery photo. I wanted to know that my father had been in the house in Sunnyvale. I wanted to know that he'd seen me, held me, and maybe even cared about me a little.

CHAPTER 26

The Life and Times of Fred Hadley

After finding Fred, I cycled through conflicting bouts of hope and dismay. I felt hopeful I had found my father, but dismayed that he was not the kind man I expected. I had to let go of the heroic Air Force pilot and beloved family man I had conjured in my imaginings, and replace that image with Fred Hadley. Fred's blogs included postings about his activities with the Wichita Lions Club and an organization called the Friendship Force, with which he'd traveled all over the world. But these posts were overshadowed by his unabashed bragging about his sexual conquests, like this example from the 1970s:

> By count, Nancy and I made love 19 times in January. Had some nooners with Sandy. Double-dipped with Sandra and Nancy the same day a number of times. Went to Derby to take care of Debra and then Nancy that night. Had Susie, for the last time, in July after taking her to a dance—also Nancy the same day [...]

A good-looking man with intense dark eyes, Fred epitomized the definition of a womanizer—a serial seducer, a man who judged women by their physical attributes and their abilities in bed. There are many synonyms for this kind of man: Casanova, Lothario, ladies' man, Don Juan, philanderer, wolf, pickup artist, and player. All of which could be used to describe him.

After reading Fred's blog I did some research on serial seducers. They are described as charming, attentive men who excel at knowing how to make women feel special, and I'm sure my young mother would have been vulnerable to that. When studying the photograph of her with the mystery man, I can see how he's giving her all his attention. How he gazes at her and holds her hand.

Sexual escapades like Fred's are not unusual among men of his type. But posting diary entries about it online did seem unusual, and troubled me. Didn't he realize anyone could read his blog? Didn't he know that those who read it would find it shocking? Or did he just not care?

I overheard Beth telling her sister about Fred's blog on the phone one day, soon after I discovered it, and I gave her a scolding look. When she ended the call I said, "I don't want people to know about that blog." I felt embarrassed by Fred's uncensored account of his life, as if it reflected badly upon *me* somehow. But I spent hours and hours reading it, amazed at the wealth of information it provided.

Fred Hadley served in the Navy from 1940 to 1946, attaining the rank of chief petty officer. He married his high school sweetheart in 1944, had a son, Fred Jr., and then met his second wife while at the University of Denver—a girl he describes as being "hot and ready." He married his second wife in 1949 and had a second son, Steve. This marriage lasted until 1962, to be followed by four more marriages and who knows how many affairs.

In addition to Fred's blog, he also posted some of his home movies on YouTube. He definitely seemed inclined to document his life. (Could this be a heritable trait?) And it wasn't all about sex. He took a lot of photographs, played golf, played chess, went to the theater, enjoyed spending time at his lakefront property, and traveled extensively, including trips to China and Russia.

In spite of my initial distaste for Fred's womanizing ways, I slowly began to appreciate his positive qualities. He was educated, professional, handsome, outgoing. I began to think I might have enjoyed his company if we had known one another over the years. And I felt grateful he was still alive.

Fred's parents met in 1920 at the Union Station train depot in Wichita, where they both worked in the diner. Fred's father, Ted Hadley, was just fifteen years old when he seduced Fred's mother, Lucy, by lying to her about his age. They were married that December and spent a few happy years together. Lucy gave birth to Fred in August of 1922, then to a daughter, Freida, in 1924. But soon after that, the marriage disintegrated and the young father of two disappeared.

"How can you miss something you never had?" Fred wrote about his father on his blog. But I had often heard my cousin Jane say the same exact phrase about her mother, and I knew it wasn't true.

After Ted Hadley abandoned his family, Fred's mother went to work at the Coleman lamp factory, where she made barely enough to support her two children, and had no one to help her with child care. As a result, Fred and Freida were temporarily placed in the Wichita Children's Home, which Fred wrote about on his blog:

> One Sunday, mother came to visit and brought me a box with six blocks in it. When she left, someone in authority took the blocks from me and dumped them into a pile of other blocks, noting that I should share them. I felt so hurt that "MY" blocks were taken away and I made such a fuss that punishment was due this unruly one. The punishment was to put me in a little blue dress and girls' underwear and parade me in front of the other children.

My heart broke for Fred when I read this. Who would humiliate a little boy like that? A little boy tragically separated from his mother. It made me think of Benny and Jane. I was struck by the unfortunate coincidence of young children separated from their parents on both sides of my family tree.

I did not receive a reply to the letter I sent Fred, and I felt too nervous about calling him again. I dreaded the potential rejection. "You need to just get on a plane and go out there," Beth said.

Considering Fred's advanced age, I knew I should go to Wichita as soon as I could. Even if it turned out that he wasn't my father, there was a chance he was my brother. Since Fred's father, Ted, had lived in Las Vegas, *he* might have been the one who knew my mother. Ted had been forty-nine when my twenty-two-year-old mother became pregnant, but I couldn't rule out the possibility.

My sons, of course, were highly interested in all of this. When I told them I might fly down to Wichita, Jeremy said he had a week off in August and wanted to go with me. I began to make plans for the trip but wanted to make sure we'd be welcome. After two weeks went by with no word from Fred, I wrote him another letter. "As I continue to research the Hadley family tree, I have come to be certain that you are either my cousin, my brother, or my father. And I would like to meet you."

While waiting to see if I would get a response to this letter, I absorbed myself in research. I found out as much as I could about Fred's sister, Freida, and his son, Fred Jr., who both lived in Wichita. I also looked up as many Hadley family members as I could on Google and Facebook and continued to work on my Hadley family tree on Ancestry.com.

When another week went by with no reply from Fred, I felt I had to call again, but I feared going through with it. What if my letters had annoyed him? What if he told me to just leave him alone? What would I do then?

I dialed his number and felt relieved to get his voice mail. I left a message and then decided to call his son, Fred Jr., who turned out to be none other than "Catarand"—the Ancestry.com user who never replied to my messages. Fred Jr. didn't seem at all surprised to get a call from a stranger who might be his sister. He told me Fred had not been feeling well lately, and not to take the lack of communication personally.

After that brief phone call, I called Fred's sister, Freida, a lively sounding ninety-year-old. Freida didn't quite understand how DNA tests had led me to the Hadley family, but she readily accepted me as a relative. She had no trouble with the idea that either Fred or Ted had fathered a long lost child.

Freida told me that Fred could hardly walk, and his kidneys were failing. "He went to the doctor on Friday and finally got on a pill for depression. You know I think that's why he's been sleeping so much lately." Freida spoke rapidly, and I took notes as fast as I could. She told me Fred had always been handsome, but a shallow person. "We never ran around together. Never had anything in common. You know, my people are good people. He's just…different."

I learned that Fred had lost an eye and now wore an eye patch. Freida described his companion, Sandy, as a good person, but brain-damaged because of an accident and on a lot of medication. Freida thought Fred should be in assisted living, but Sandy didn't want him to go. I had just joined the family and already there was family drama.

A widow, Freida lived on her own in a retirement village called Presbyterian Manor. She had just given up her car but had a granddaughter who came once a week to take her out. At the end of our first phone call, I felt lucky to be related to someone as friendly as Freida. I immediately wrote her a letter and included photos of myself and my sons.

The day after I talked to Freida, I got an e-mail message from one of the California Hadley's who had just gotten the results of her DNA test at Ancestry. The daughter of one of Fred's cousins, she matched me as a second cousin. Not a big surprise.

I knew I had found my paternal family, and most likely my father, but I could not quite believe I had done it. If I had suddenly learned to play the cello, with my feet, I would not have been more amazed. Yet it was such an ordinary thing—to know one's own family.

I booked a flight to Wichita and began to make plans for the trip. I called Freida to let her know when I'd be there, and while we were talking I asked if she would be willing to take a DNA test. I had to explain DNA testing to her again, and although she still did not quite understand it, she agreed. If she matched me as a cousin, I would know that my father was *not* Fred or Ted. But if she matched me as an aunt or half-sister, I would know for sure. I paid for a DNA test kit that would be mailed to her address, but since Freida did not have a computer, the results would be attached to my online account.

Freida told me that Fred had recently been taken to the hospital by ambulance. He'd had a fever, couldn't swallow, and his companion, Sandy, couldn't move him herself. Arrangements were made for Fred to go into a nursing home, but he refused, so Fred Jr. went to the hospital and drove him home. "He's doing better now," Freida said. "He's eating."

I wondered if Fred would be well enough to meet me when I got to Wichita. "I don't know that they'll invite you into the house," Freida said.

That same day, I talked to Fred's son Steve Hadley. Freida described Steve as "so smart and so handsome," but alluded to some questionable choices he'd made in life. I got the impression that Steve was the black sheep of the family, at least in Freida's estimation. He lived in Texas and worked as a roof inspector.

I called Steve, told him my story, told him I'd talked to Fred, Fred Jr., and Freida. I told him about the DNA tests and the cousins and Las Vegas and the photo of the mystery man. "Wow," he said a few times. Our conversation left me feeling unsure about how I had been received. After we talked, I sent him an e-mail and anxiously awaited a reply.

While all these amazing events were happening, regular life as I know it carried on. Beth and I were away from home quite a bit that summer. We went on a cruise to the Bahamas, drove to Washington, D.C. for a wedding, spent two weeks at Lake Michigan, had a week-long visit with the grandkids, and went to Beth's family reunion. In addition, I led a memoir-writing workshop and endured several small disasters. Our basement flooded due to a torrential rainstorm, my laptop died, and my phone was murdered by a hot grease splatter. It was the best of times, it was the worst of times. I often felt overwhelmed. The day I accidentally downloaded malware onto my brand-new laptop, I almost lost my mind.

When I finally received an e-mail reply from Steve Hadley, I got a little teary-eyed at what he had to say: "I hope that Dad will agree to your visit, but he is still weak, and having company of any sort might be a bit much." Steve warned me about Sandy, describing her as "an obstacle of sorts." And at the end of his message he wrote, "If you have any questions about Dad, please feel free to call or write. We could spend a good deal of time catching up on each other's lives; isn't that what long lost half siblings should do?"

I felt tremendously relieved by the acceptance I received from my new relatives, but I proceeded with caution, as if they were woodland creatures who might suddenly get spooked and hop away, or turn into hissing cats with claws, like my aunt Chris in Bristol.

In my next e-mail to Steve, I attached a photo of the mystery man. He wrote back saying he did not think the man was Fred. I also sent a copy of the mystery man photo to Freida, who said the same thing. But even if Fred was *not* the mystery man, that didn't mean he was not my father.

I talked to Freida again after she received my letter with the photos enclosed.

"You have my dimples!" she said.

There were many things Freida told me about herself that could also describe me—funny little similarities that made me smile. "I've never been bored," she said. "I keep records on everything... I have a hard time making decisions... My big thing is researching illnesses... I have to know everything about everything... I love to dance... I've started groups all my life."

She told me that Fred felt much better and was getting around. She had talked to him recently and said he sounded like himself again. But she had also talked to Sandy, who said, "Fred doesn't want that woman coming around." Meaning me.

Four days before my trip to Wichita I got a call from Freida. She had changed her mind and did not want to do the DNA test. Her grandchildren had become alarmed when they heard about a stranger who had been calling her, and wanted a sample of her cells.

I couldn't blame them for being cautious. I downplayed my disappointment, told Freida we would decide what to do with the DNA test kit when I got there. Maybe Fred Jr. would be willing to take it.

I planned the trip to Wichita knowing I might not get to meet Fred Sr., and I was okay with that. Considering Fred's age, his illness, and his unstable companion, meeting him seemed unlikely. But just in case, I purchased an over-the-counter paternity test at the drugstore and packed it in my bag.

CHAPTER 27

Wichita

I had never been to the state of Kansas and never expected to go there for any reason. I imagined Kansas as a flat, empty, featureless place, square in shape and square in character, and this turned out to be true, at least for the small part of it I visited.

When we arrived, Jeremy and I rented a car and drove to our motel, a threadbare place with extended-stay suites. Temperatures were in the high nineties, but I felt enormously alert in spite of the heat. In addition to the exciting prospect of meeting my paternal relatives, the opportunity to travel with my adult son made the trip especially pleasurable for me.

At the age of thirty-three, Jeremy and Justin were both busily involved in their lives in Kalamazoo. We didn't see each other often, and I felt lucky if I talked to them once a week. Jeremy had recently returned to college in pursuit of a business degree, and also worked full time. He had planned a vacation trip with his girlfriend for August, but they broke up and he had the time free. The stars aligned. I can't imagine another scenario where I would have a chance to spend four days with one of my sons, just the two of us.

Jeremy and I settled in, went out to dinner, and then I called Fred Jr. to ask if it would be okay for us to come by that evening. He said sure, and it didn't take long to get to his ranch-style house in a rural area just outside of town.

The house sat on an unremarkable corner at the intersection of two flat country roads. I felt more curious than nervous as we approached the front door, which was opened by Fred Jr.'s wife, Cindy, before we could knock. We were greeted warmly by Cindy and then by Fred Jr. "Well, hello!" he said. I shook his hand and stared at him, a hefty man with a scraggly beard and white hair. I zeroed in on his features, searching for recognition, for some kind of sign we could be siblings. Although I moved and spoke normally, the neurons in my brain were firing like crazy. Fred Jr. and I kept meeting each other's eyes and then quickly looking away.

Jeremy and I were invited into the tidy, sparsely furnished living room, which looked like nothing in it had changed since sometime in the 1980s, including the wallpaper and carpeting. Jeremy and I sat on the couch, which was upholstered in a brownish patterned plush fabric, and Fred Jr. sat in the matching chair. Cindy, who struck me as being especially kind and good-natured, carried a kitchen chair into the room for herself. I got the impression they did not receive many visitors.

I was struck by Fred Jr.'s resemblance to Fred Sr., and also by the similarity of their voices. Fred Jr. talked slowly and punctuated his speech with exaggerated facial expressions. He had majored in math in college and worked at Boeing in IT until his retirement. He told us he had been shy all his life and did not enjoy attending family gatherings. As he talked to us about Fred Sr., I came to understand that they were not particularly close.

Fred Jr. was not the kind of sophisticated sibling I had hoped for in my family romance fantasies, but I felt an instant fondness for him. He told us about some serious medical issues he had recently experienced and shared what he knew about the Hadley family history. He invited us into his dusty home office, where he fired up his desktop computer and gave us a tour of his family tree online. Soon after that, we said our goodbyes. We hugged each other and promised to stay in touch.

The next day, we drove over to Presbyterian Manor to have lunch with Freida. "Oh my, you're both so tall," she said when we arrived at her tiny apartment. At six foot five, Jeremy looked gigantic next to Freida, who turned out to be much smaller than I expected. Wearing a cranberry tunic top and white slacks, she looked awfully good for ninety. We had hardly said our hellos when she handed me an eight-by-ten photo of Ted Hadley standing in a restaurant with eight pretty girls. Freida felt certain that one of the girls would turn out to be my mother and that would be that, mystery solved. I hated to disappoint her, but Ann was not in the photo. "Well, shoot," she said.

She hustled us out of her apartment and down a long hall that led to the manor's dining room, a large but not especially cheery place. We sat at a round table with two of her neighbors and chatted throughout the bland lunch. Jeremy and I were both on our best, most charming behavior. Freida asked me to explain to her neighbors about how I had found her through DNA, and they were all fascinated by that. Jeremy talked about his interest in meeting biological relatives since all of his grandparents, except Ann Preston, were unknown. "Every time I go to the doctor and they ask about my family medical history, I have to say, 'I don't know,'" he said.

After lunch, we returned to Freida's apartment, where we spent the next four hours. We sat at her table as she showed us her photo albums and told us her stories. Freida tended to think Ted was most likely my father because he lived in Las Vegas, but I felt sure it was Fred because of the age difference. "What's your blood type," Freida asked. When I said B positive she beamed and said, "Me, too!" She gave me a handful of photos of Ted and Fred to take with me, and then surprised me by agreeing to take the DNA test after all.

I guided her through the process of collecting the samples of cells from her cheeks, which is done with swabs that come in the kit. In just a few minutes, I had in my possession an envelope containing moist Q-tips that potentially held the key to my identity.

After thanking Freida profusely and hugging her goodbye, Jeremy and I drove into downtown Wichita, found a bar, and ordered ourselves some celebratory drinks. I felt tremendously relieved, tremendously hopeful, and so glad I had come to Kansas. I called Fred Sr. that evening and left a message saying I was in town and would like to meet him.

After breakfast the next morning, I got a call from Fred Jr. He had just received a call from Fred Sr. saying he wanted to meet us, but not at his house. So we made a plan to meet in a restaurant, a place called Piccadilly's, in a half hour. *A half hour!* This all happened so suddenly I misplaced my phone while rushing around to get ready, and my hands shook so much I could hardly get my earrings in.

We drove to the restaurant, not far from our motel, and took a seat in a booth. A few moments later, Fred Jr. walked in from the lobby and glanced around. He spotted me, waved, and then went back out. I got up and walked into the lobby just as Fred Jr. assisted Fred Sr. out of the car he had parked at the restaurant entrance. I stepped forward, introduced myself, and asked Fred Sr. if I could give him a hand. "I wish you would," he said. I reached out to take Fred's arm, but he took my hand instead and we began to walk slowly toward the booth.

I had been prepared to meet an old man, but I didn't realize how small and frail Fred would be. He shuffled along in his baggy slacks and zipped-up black fleece jacket. I had a hard time equating him with the man who had written that blog. That handsome Lothario. I have never experienced a more surreal moment than to be walking along, holding hands in an intimately familiar way with a man who could be my father. The walk to the booth took a long time, and also seemed to happen quite quickly.

Fred Sr. sat across from Jeremy, and Fred Jr. sat across from me. When the waitress came over, Fred Sr. ordered a beer, which he had a hard time lifting from the table. When he finally succeeded, I toasted him with my iced tea. He smiled a lot but didn't talk much, and when he did he spoke softly. He kept looking into my eyes, which I'm sure had been his modus operandi with countless women, but seemed meaningful to me just the same.

At one point I said, "I think I have your eyes, Fred."

"Yes. I think you do," he said.

I didn't badger Fred Sr. with questions about his possible paternity; we simply had a nice visit. Jeremy and Fred Jr. did most of the talking. We discussed the weather, the aircraft industry, the world travels of Fred Sr., Lake Michigan, and the place Fred Sr. once owned on Grand Lake in Oklahoma. "I wish I was there now," he said. We hadn't been visiting long, maybe fifteen or twenty minutes, when Fred Sr. asked for the check. He paid by credit card, and it took an excruciatingly long time for him to sign the bill.

I escorted Fred back to the door, holding hands once again. On the way he said that getting old was a terrible thing and I really ought to avoid it. We sat on a bench in the lobby while we waited for Fred Jr. to get the car. I sat close to Fred for a photo that Jeremy took, and then I helped him to the car and we said goodbye.

The visit with Fred came and went so suddenly, it took a while for me to comprehend that it had happened. I had worried needlessly about being rejected. *What a relief!* I felt delighted, lucky, and enormously cheerful. That afternoon, Jeremy and I met with my cousin Barbie Hamlin in another local restaurant, and later that evening we met with Fred Jr.'s son, Michael. Michael came to our motel to meet us and brought along his young daughter, Ella. They both immediately felt like family to me, especially Ella with her big brown eyes. We hung out at the motel pool and talked until dark.

On our last day in town, Jeremy and I went to see Wichita's most iconic image, the *Keeper of the Plains*, a Native American sculpture overlooking the Arkansas River. Wichita turned out to be more interesting than I expected, but not a place I would want to stay for long. Although I felt a connection with the family members I met there, Wichita seemed foreign to me. Landlocked in the middle of the country, it felt confining and remote. I clicked my heels together, like that Kansas girl Dorothy, and gladly went *home* to Detroit.

CHAPTER 28

An Incredible Thing

After the trip to Wichita, I got an e-mail from Steve Hadley letting me know that Fred Sr. had checked into a physical-rehabilitation facility the day after I met him.

> I think Dad didn't want anyone to come to his house because Sandy was there. Otherwise your visit with Dad could have lasted much longer, and would have been much easier on him. I'm not sure if he checked into the rehab so he can get help getting stronger, or if he just wanted to get away from Sandy for a while.

Steve gave me Fred's phone number at the rehab and suggested I call. "I think he would be glad to hear from you." I felt nervous about talking to Fred. I worried about making a good impression in a way that felt like the beginning of a romantic relationship, or maybe a job interview. But when I worked up the nerve to call, Fred did indeed seem happy to hear from me.

"How is your quest going?" he asked.

I told him we'd have the results of Freida's test in a few weeks, "and then we'll know."

"And then we'll know," he repeated.

I asked him if he'd ever been to Sunnyvale, and he said he didn't think so. He also said, "I don't think that's me," in reference to the photo of the mystery man with my mother. He said how sorry he was that I had lost my mother. And then we ended up talking about his time in the Navy, about Hawaii and Fiji. He told me he had written a column for the Navy-base paper on Hawaii, the *Kaneohe Klipper*. "It was all about what was going on around the base."

I told him that sounded like the kind of thing I would have done. "I've written columns for newspapers, too."

"Well how about that," he said.

I found myself becoming fond of Fred. I enjoyed talking to him but had to speak slowly and louder than normal in order to be understood. I had to repeat myself frequently, which hampered the communication process. We hadn't talked for long before Fred tired out.

I sent him a card for his birthday at the end of August, and in early September I got an e-mail from Steve. He told me Fred had come home from rehab and felt much better, but he was fighting with Sandy. She stopped making his meals, and so Fred *drove* himself to I-Hop for a waffle. He also drove to the country club near his home a couple of times.

Good for him, I thought. I appreciated Fred's independent spirit, even though it shocked me to imagine him on the road.

A few weeks later I got the results of Freida's DNA test. She matched me as either an aunt or half-sister, confirming that my father had to be either Fred or Ted, and I literally let out a long sigh of relief. *I wasn't barking up the wrong tree!* I knew. For sure. My father was definitely one of two men.

When a person submits his or her DNA for analysis and then compares it to the DNA of another, the results come in the form of a number that predicts their potential relationship. A parent and child would share approximately 3400 centiMorgans of autosomal DNA. Full siblings would share about 2640. If two people share about 1700, then their relationship is either grandparent to grandchild, aunt or uncle to niece or nephew, or half siblings. Freida and I share 1761 centiMorgans of autosomal DNA, quite a bit more than my second closest match, my cousin Laura Harper, with whom I share only 222.

As soon as I got the results, I called Freida, Fred Jr., and Steve to tell them the news. They all seemed quite unsurprised. I also called Fred to ask if he would be willing to take a paternity test, and he readily agreed. I still had the paternity-testing kit I had purchased at the drugstore before the trip to Wichita. I read the directions and typed them out for Fred in 16-point font. He would need to swab his cheeks with the big swabs, put them into the envelope included with the kit, and mail it back to me in the self-addressed envelope I provided. I would then add my own cheek swabs before mailing the kit to the lab.

A week later I got a phone message from Fred. "Something terrible has happened," he said. "The envelope you sent me with all the swabs in it, and all the instructions, has disappeared." He said he put the envelope on his kitchen table, but when he went to do the test he couldn't find it. "Maybe the dog ate it," he said, inferring that maybe Sandy disposed of it. I could hear her bitching in the background as Fred recorded his message. "So, Hilary, what we need to do is have you send another package. I'll be waiting to hear from you and hopefully we can get our lineage straightened out."

I called Fred back as soon as I got his message and told him I would send another set of swabs and instructions right away. He said he'd do the new test as soon as he got it. "I'll do it right that instant." He also said he hoped he was my father, "because you're a lovely person and I love you."

I sent Fred a new kit and then called him a few days later to see if he had mailed it back to me yet. He confirmed that he had. "Special delivery," he said. And then he told me, again, how he hoped he was my father, and that he felt sorry for all the time we had missed.

I didn't know how to take this. It overwhelmed me to hear my potential father say these things. It went way beyond anything I had ever imagined in my most hopeful reunion fantasies. And from Fred, I didn't quite trust it. I knew it was probably just the sweet talk of an old charmer. But that didn't keep me from being charmed.

Two weeks later, I received Fred's paternity-test results, which came to me in an e-mail. I opened it and found my Personal Paternity Analysis Report. "Conclusion: Fred C. Hadley is excluded as the biological father of Hilary A. Harper." A chart followed this blunt message showing the significant places in our "genetic systems" that did not match. Fred's probability of paternity: 0 percent.

I sat looking at this e-mail on my laptop for several long minutes, trying to figure out how this could be. It took a while before I realized what this meant.

Fred was my brother. Ted was my father.

Ted was my father.

An incredible thing had just happened: I *knew* the identity of my father. I had an answer to the question I'd been asking for such a long time. Yet I felt let down. I didn't know anything about Ted. And he wasn't alive.

I got up from my desk and walked around the house with my hand clasped over my heart. I couldn't sit down. I had to move and do things. I called Beth but don't remember what we said. I put dishes into the dishwasher. Sent texts to my sons. All my work had finally paid off, but I only felt a numb kind of shock.

When I looked at myself in the bathroom mirror, I looked for Ted and couldn't see him, except in my eyes, which I now knew were *his*. I went into my office to look at the photos Freida had given me. I had six photos of Ted in my possession, plus several more on Fred's blog. In every one Ted has a moustache, thin in the 1940s, full in the 1970s. A handsome man, with his dark hair combed straight back, he is wearing a suit in nearly every photo, and in every photo he is smiling.

When I called Fred that evening to tell him the news, he said, "Well, hell."

I asked him what he knew about Ted and he said, "Not much." He said he had only met Ted a handful of times.

Some of the photos of Ted, which I saw in Freida's scrapbook, were taken in Los Angeles in the 1940s. In them, Ted looks as attractive as any movie star of the era. Later in his life, when

he lived in Las Vegas, Ted appeared on a children's television show. Freida gave me a copy of a newspaper article about this TV show, which included a photo of Ted in costume as his character, "Pedro."

This led me to have a hunch about Ted.

"Do you think he wanted to be an actor?" I asked Fred.

"Oh yeah. He told me he'd been a stand-in for Clark Gable. But my mother said, 'Don't believe a word he says.'"

I told Fred how disappointed I felt to get the results of the paternity test, and he agreed. He said he would have been glad to have me for a daughter. "Especially because you're so smart and nice."

"Aw, Fred, that's sweet," I said, without a doubt of his sincerity.

"So, what are you doing tonight?" he asked.

"I'm just trying to absorb this new information," I said. "How about you?"

He said he was reading the paper, which led to a discussion of the comic pages and what our favorite comics were. He liked *Dilbert* and *Herman*, and this mundane conversation seemed remarkable to me. My *brother* and I were talking about a simple thing we both enjoyed.

At the end of our conversation that night I said, "Okay then, Fred, goodnight, I love you."

"I love you, too," he said.

My feelings for Fred had gone from disgust to affection in a short amount of time. It felt odd to have a ninety-two-year-old sibling, but that's how it worked out since our father was seventeen when Fred was born and forty-nine at the time of my birth.

Among the diary entries Fred has posted on his blog, there is this one, written on January 1, 1940 when he was a high school senior:

This morning about 11:30 Ted (my dad) came. The first time in 11 years. We went and got Pat and rode around in his '38 Pontiac. [...] He has a mustash and is very good looking. He said that he would like to take us to Phoenix Arizona with him, but maybe he is just blowing—I hope not.

Fred did not see his father again until 1944.

When I called Freida to tell her the results of the paternity test, she said, "I always thought that would be it." She told me what she could about Ted, but she hadn't spent much time with him either. "He left when I was three and didn't come back until I was sixteen."

I asked if she missed him, and she said, "I was too busy to miss him."

Freida told me she had always sent Ted a Father's Day card, "but it was hard to find one that didn't say what a great father he was."

Ted married his second wife in 1929 and settled in Los Angeles. His parents and nearly all of his siblings eventually moved from Kansas to California in the 1920s and '30s. Fred and Freida grew up in Wichita not knowing their Hadley relatives. Then, in 1942, Freida went to California to be near her fiancé, a serviceman stationed in San Diego. While there, she lived with Ted in LA for a while.

Freida remembers Ted saying that if he wanted a job in an Italian restaurant, he'd say he was Italian, and if it was a French restaurant, he'd claim to be French. Ted went to the beach every Sunday, she said, and he felt sorry for not having a better education. "He always wanted to be somebody."

CHAPTER 29

A Different Person

It took a while for the fact that I had found my father to sink in. At first, the knowledge penetrated only the surface of my comprehension. It took a few weeks before it fully saturated my consciousness—a process I have been through enough times now to recognize as a process. It seems as if the human brain needs to restructure when presented with this kind of identity-altering information. It needs to shuffle things around, create a new schematic, rewire the circuits.

I had spent two months adjusting to the concept of Fred as my father. So the sudden shift to Ted felt disconcerting. I could imagine my mother being seduced by young Fred's charms, but I had a harder time imagining her with Ted. *What was she doing with Ted?*

Ever since I first read Margaret Rutledge's letter, in which she says my mother asked "that fellow (the father)" for some money to leave Las Vegas on, I had imagined a story in which my parents knew one another over a period of some time, a few months at the least. But I doubt "that fellow" was Ted. That fellow was probably the Greek. The officer.

My mother must have believed the big Greek was my father. Ted might have just been a one-night stand. She might even have regretted her tryst with him—a forty-nine-year-old married man. When I considered this possibility in the days after getting the paternity-test results, it made me feel accidental. I felt like much more of a mistake than I had when imagining my mother having a romance with a tall, heroic jet pilot.

Shortly after learning that Ted was my father, I spent some time with Jane. I wanted to see if there were any photos of Ted in the old photo albums, and Jane let me take them home with me for a few weeks. I didn't find any evidence of Ted, but on close inspection I realized one of the albums had belonged to my mother. There are several photos inscribed to Ann within it; photos of the family who employed her as a nanny; and many other clues that this album was hers.

On one page in Ann's photo album – a page I now refer to as "the boyfriend page" – are photos of three men. Two of the photos are of young guys who appear on other pages in the album, and one is a 5X7 of a good looking man in an Air Force officer's uniform. Something had been written below this photo – in white pencil on the black paper page – and then scratched out (which is so typical of Ann.) So, of course, I wonder if this man was the "Big Greek" or maybe "Stanley." In any case, he seems to have held a prominent place in Ann's affections.

Beth seemed more delighted than me about the success of my search.

"I can't believe it," she said several times with wonder. "You did it!"

I appreciated Beth's pride in my detective skills but didn't feel the happiness you would expect of someone in my shoes. It all seemed rather anticlimactic at first.

Thankfully, my dulled emotions did not persist. The shock wore off, my brain adapted, and the more I learned about Ted Hadley, the better I felt about inheriting his genes. I set to work finding out as much about my father as I could, and discovered quite a bit.

Elda Theodore Hadley was born in 1905 in Kansas City, the tenth of twelve children. He grew up on a farm and left home at the age of fourteen. In the 1920 census, he gave his name as Theo. His residence that year is listed as a rooming house in Wichita, his occupation as dishwasher in a hotel. Why he left home at fourteen and went to work, I'll never know.

At the age of fifteen, while working at the Harvey House lunchroom in the Wichita train station, Ted met and married a pretty twenty-year-old named Lucy to whom he lied about his age. By the time he was nineteen he had two children, Fred and Freida. Sometime after Freida's birth, Ted left Lucy, leading to a lot of hardship and heartache before they finally divorced.

Ted wrote letters to Lucy while they were separated, letters which still exist and which I now, incredibly, have in my possession thanks to Freida's generosity. She mailed them to me a few weeks after I got the news.

In a letter dated 1925, Ted wrote to Lucy: "Honey, we must keep the kids together so they will be happy. If you think we cannot get along, let's just quit for two or three months."

In November of 1926, he wrote to Lucy from Oklahoma City:

To the sweetest girl in the world—my little doll. How are you? And all my family? …I will do just as you say. Or anything you say. But right now I am trying to save some money. I will be back before long and have a good job. Honey did you ever sit down and think about all the things you and I have gone through? Do you remember the first night? Every time I think about those things I cry and cry. I don't know why. But I guess just because I love you so much. I sure am lonesome for the kids. Will have lots of things for Xmas, maybe be Santa Claus.

In 1927, Ted spent some time in jail for abandonment. While incarcerated, he wrote letters to Lucy in pencil on cheap brown paper: "My Dear Girl, what you are doing will never do anyone any good. And I am sure it is not you who is doing this. Because I know you think more of me than to have our children's father a convict. Or is this what you want?"

In another letter he wrote, "Why don't you come see me? Just to see you would do me a lot of good. No one has come to see me and it sure gets lonesome. I can't blame you for wanting to go ahead, and I will admit I told lies. So if you can't believe me now, I guess it is my hard luck."

In 1929, Ted married his second wife, Ruth. Ted and Ruth went to Los Angeles for their honeymoon and decided to make it their home. In the 1930 census, Ted's occupation is listed as "manager of a café." Ted was twenty-five that year. Ruth, twenty-three.

In 1937, Ted and Ruth had a daughter, Barbara, who lives near San Diego, California. We began to get to know one another a few weeks after I learned we share a father, and she turned out to be a bountiful source of information. During several long telephone conversations with Barb, I took pages and pages of notes.

"I never saw my dad mad or angry," she said. She told me Ted had some friends who owned a restaurant and hotel in LA and that he worked for them for many years. "He was a very hard worker," she said. "He had a strong work ethic." She told me he wasn't a drinker, had a great sense of humor, and was also a photographer. "He developed photos in pans in the bathroom," she said.

I asked Barb if she thought Ted wanted to be an actor and she said, "Oh yes. He loved being the center of attention. He was very charismatic."

Barb's parents separated in 1943, when she was seven years old. Ted married his third wife, Helen, in 1944, a glamorous woman who had once been part of a singing sister act. There is a photo of Ted and Helen in the 1940s that looks like a movie still. They were both such strikingly good-looking people, they could have been Gable and Lombard.

In 1946, Barb's mother took a job somewhere "far away" (Barb doesn't remember where). Because of this, Barb went to live with Ted and Helen in Redondo Beach. She lived with them for two years and saw her mother only twice in that time, but didn't mind because Redondo Beach was such a great place to live: "We lived right across the street from the beach."

Barb fondly recalls learning to swim in the ocean and riding inner tubes on the waves. She said she liked living with Ted and

Helen because they were so much fun. "They knew so many wonderful people, and did so many wonderful things."

In 1948, Ted and Helen left LA, and so Barb went to live with her uncle Herb, Ted's older brother. Barb described Herb as outgoing and personable. "Those Hadley brothers were all like that," she said, "very charming. But Dad could top them all."

Barb's mother returned to Southern California in 1949 and reunited with her daughter. They lived together in an apartment, where Ted would frequently show up "out of the blue." Barb recalls Ted tossing silver dollars to her. She could keep as many as she could catch. When he left he'd say, "It's time to go back up the hill." Which meant, back to Las Vegas.

Barb graduated from high school in 1954, the year I was born. She spent that summer with Ted in Nevada. It surprised me to learn that Ted owned or managed (Barb isn't sure which) a restaurant in Indian Springs, a tiny locale forty-five miles northwest of Las Vegas.

Indian Springs is not a town. Officially, it is a "census-designated place." A ramshackle hamlet surrounded by desert and top-secret military installations. Business was booming in Indian Springs in the early 1950s due to the testing of atomic bombs, which occurred nearby on the Nevada Proving Grounds. The proving grounds employed thousands of people, many of whom no doubt frequented the establishments in Indian Springs, along with curious civilians.

More than one hundred nuclear bombs were exploded in the Nevada desert in the 1950s, and the mushroom clouds they produced became an attraction for tourists. The Las Vegas Chamber of

Commerce printed calendars advertising detonation times and the best viewing locations. Barb didn't see any nuclear explosions during her summer in Indian Springs, but she did hear a few of them.

"I thought I was going to have fun with all those Air Force boys," Barb said, "but Dad handed me a menu and put me to work." The restaurant Ted ran was called the Oasis, and it had a great jukebox. "There was a gas station and a motel next door, but not much else."

This information made me wonder how my mother and Ted met. I felt sure that Ann worked somewhere on Fremont Street or the strip. So, if Ted was out in Indian Springs, how would they have known one another?

Barb told me that Ted often went into Las Vegas to get supplies for the Oasis. She went along with him a couple of times. She said they went to a place near the railroad tracks on Fremont Street. "There was a hotel there that Ted liked to go to."

I knew the place Barb meant. When I visited Fremont Street in 2007, I took photos of it. Now known as the Golden Gate Casino Hotel, in the 1950s it was called the Sal Sagev, Las Vegas spelled backward. Located at the western end of Fremont, across the street from what was once the Union Pacific train depot, it is a landmark that has stood on that corner since 1906. Their slogan is, "What happens in Vegas started here."

I remember standing on Fremont Street, studying that hotel, wondering if my mother had spent any time there. I wondered if she had taken the train from San Francisco to Las Vegas, and if this building had been one of the first things she saw when she arrived. Maybe my mother worked in that hotel. And maybe Ted met her there, in the bar or the coffee shop. Her English accent probably fascinated him, and she, no doubt, felt flattered by his charm and good looks.

In subsequent conversations, Barb told me she didn't think the hotel was the Sal Sagev. She said it could have been the El Cortez. Or maybe the Golden Nugget. Or maybe it doesn't matter. They met. And apparently hit it off.

During the time he knew my mother, Ted was appearing on a local television show for children. The *Bostick Wester Ranger* show aired live in Las Vegas beginning in July of 1953. The star of the show, Bostick Wester, was a former radio personality known for his many character voices. During the half-hour cowboy-themed show, Wester would talk to kids in the studio audience about the West and horses. Ted, wearing a Mexican cowboy outfit, played Bostick's sidekick, Pedro.

I did as much research as I could about the show, but I'm not sure how long it ran or how long Ted appeared on it. The show quickly grew in popularity until just about every kid in Las Vegas was a Bostick Wester Ranger, and I'm sure Ted enjoyed this modicum of fame.

In one of the photographs Freida gave me, Ted is riding a donkey in his Pedro costume. On the back of this photo he wrote, "This is why I did not make it to Wichita," which makes me smile every time I read it. I love the way this reveals Ted's sense of humor, and how it makes him come alive for me.

In spite of feeling a little embarrassed for Ted, a grown man dressed in a ridiculous outfit—so silly in his big sombrero—and probably doing a cringe-worthy caricature of a Mexican, I'm glad to know he finally got an acting gig.

One day during Barb's stay with Ted and Helen in the summer of 1954, they went to a radio station where a man was broadcasting. Barb had never been inside a radio studio and found it fascinating, but doesn't remember why they were there or the broadcaster's name.

"They knew *all* those people," she said about Ted and Helen.

The man at the radio station could have been Bostick Wester. Or maybe it was Jack Kogan? Considering that both Wester and Kogan were radio personalities, perhaps they knew one another. And perhaps this had something to do with how my mother and Ted knew one another.

Did Ted take the photograph of my mother with Jack Kogan?

Maybe Ted, a guy who developed photographs in his sink, took the photo as a favor to Kogan, using my mother, a pretty young waitress, as a model. Or maybe he took the photo of my mother with Kogan as a way to impress her, then gave her the print as a gift.

Either scenario is plausible. And it pleased me to realize, after so many years of imagining my father taking this photograph, that I might be right about that, after all. Even though I'll never know for sure, and I'll never know the whole story, I know enough to satisfy my curiosity.

Barb went to Las Vegas for New Year's Eve in December of 1954 and she remembers Ted working at the Silver Slipper casino at that time. So, who knows what happened to the Oasis. Maybe Ted got tired of the commute. In 1958, Ted married his fourth wife, Leona, about whom I know nothing. Then in 1967, at the age of sixty-two, he married his fifth wife, Lucienne, a French Canadian who worked as a wardrobe mistress at the Tropicana. Ted and Lucienne remained together until his death in 1990.

Ted spent the last few years of his life in a nursing home in Costa Mesa, California. Barb visited him there several times, but was not told of his death when it happened. Lucienne took care of the details of having Ted cremated and interring his ashes, but did not inform his family. Barb learned that Ted had died when she went to visit him one day.

"I was so shocked," she said.

In November of 2014, Barb sent me a DVD compilation of home movies Ted took in the early 1940s. Originally spliced together onto one big reel by Ted himself, the movies reveal him as a lighthearted, goofy ham of a guy. Ted, his siblings, and their families look to have been quite a fun bunch. Everyone seems to be having a good time. The reel includes several scenes of Ted displaying his dramatic ability. On the beach, he pretends to be crawling across a desert, dying of thirst. In another scene he is some sort of monstrous creature. In yet another, he expressively raises one eyebrow—a talent my sons and my grandson also have.

When the DVD arrived in the mail, I watched it immediately, astonished to see my paternal grandparents on film, along with many of my aunts and uncles. Here they were. My *family*. My people. I watched Ted's movie and realized that this is what the search had been all about, to see the faces of my relatives, to know something about them, and to understand: this is why I am who I am.

The way I comprehend myself has changed since finding Ted. I am now able to take what I know about the Prestons, mix it with what I know about the Hadleys, and see how this results in me being me. It's wonderful to look in the mirror and not see a mystery.

I feel like a different person, an oddly more confident person. I am more at *ease* with myself. And I am at peace. I didn't realize how bothersome the unknown part of myself had been until it no longer felt bothersome. Like an ache that suddenly subsides.

I also feel glad my father turned out to be an okay guy. Not the guy I expected him to be, and certainly flawed, but flawed in a way I can understand. I *get* Ted Hadley. And as a result, I more completely *get* myself.

It seems funny to me now that I wished my father to be a military hero and an upstanding family man. That would not have suited me at all. I'm glad to know that Ted was an unconventional character. An actor at heart. A photographer. A guy who loved the beach and longed to *be* someone. I wish I could have had the chance to go to the movies with him, to have made a meal with him, told him a joke, and taken his picture.

Soon after learning that Ted is my father, Fred sent me a DVD copy of a video he made in 1986. Taken during a visit to Ted's nursing-home room in Costa Mesa, it is a heartbreaking documentation. Ted appears to be in bad shape, grimacing in pain and occasionally confused. "Are we in Wichita?" he asks at one point.

The home movies Ted made are silent, so hearing his voice on Fred's DVD was a remarkable experience for me. Unfortunately, most of the video is dominated by Ted's wife, Lucienne, who rarely stops talking. Fred is able to converse with Ted only during the few times Lucienne leaves the room. It is during these brief conversations that hints of the man Ted had been become evident. When asked why he spent so much of his life in Las Vegas, he says, "That's where the money was." And when Fred recalls Ted's beef stroganoff, Ted explains that you have to take the fat off a side of New York strip and then cut it across the grain.

Fred asks Ted if he remembers a family reunion that took place in Wichita in 1975. "We got a picture of you with your children, grandchildren, and great-grandchildren," Fred says.

"Yeah," Ted says sadly, then wipes at tears in his eyes.

Ted Hadley, Venice Beach pier, 1930

EPILOGUE

People who search for unknown family members no longer have to go through what I went through: the erroneous clues, the flawed assumptions, the dead ends. Genetic genealogy has changed all that. Now anyone can find their relatives with just a little bit of luck and logic. All it takes is a few good cousin matches from a DNA database, plus the ability to understand and build family trees. I got lucky in that respect. Dogged determination helped, too.

Not long after finding Ted, I gave DNA test kits to my sons, which eventually led to the identity of Mike's biological parents. Both of Mike's parents were deceased by the time I found them, but I also found his full sister living in Grand Rapids, and two half siblings in Chicago. In spite of his reticence to search, Mike was grateful to finally know his parents' names, to see their photos, and to meet his sister, Kay, who was also given up for adoption at birth, one year before him.

Best of all, our sons now have a complete family tree—the most meaningful gift I ever gave them. Jeremy said, "You've got mad skills, Mom," in reference to my search abilities, and that is the most gratifying compliment I ever received.

Beth and I were married in Chicago in April of 2015. Our brief ceremony took place at the Cook County Marriage Court. A joyous day. We had a wedding reception a month later, complete with a tiered cake and a strolling accordionist.

That summer we traveled to Wichita together to visit Freida and meet more of my extended Hadley family. And then, in September, I flew to California where I met my half-sister Barbara, my niece Cheryl, and my cousin Pam Farrow.

California is even more mythic in significance to me now, a place that connects me to both my mother and my father. While walking along the shore of the Pacific I felt a deep sense of satisfaction. All my questions had been answered and my story had been told.

A NOTE FROM THE AUTHOR

All the events in this memoir have been told as I remember them occurring. The names of some individuals have been changed in order to protect their privacy.

I hope you enjoyed reading this memoir. If you did, please tell a friend, share it on social media, and post a few kind words on Goodreads or Amazon.

Thanks, so much!

Hilary Harper

Website: hilaryharper.net
Facebook: facebook.com/hilaryharperauthor
Instagram: instagram.com/hilarywho44

ACKNOWLEDGEMENTS

Thanks to those who gave good notes along the way: Margery Guest, Catherine Frericks, Marti Ayres White, Jean Reed Bahle, Diane Wendover Valilee, Maryjane Pories, Betsy Emdin, Karen Hildebrant, Lori Eaton, Alex Morgan, Anne Osmer, Joan Elmucci, Sandra Karolak, my podmates at Queens, Jane Alison, Kathryn Rhett, and Beth Baumgartner. Thanks also to Kazuo Ishiguro for permission to quote from his work, and to James Kao, for allowing the use of his photograph.

CPSIA information can be obtained
at www.ICGtesting.com
Printed in the USA
LVHW031720260819
628958LV00005B/804/P

9 780998 626208